D0953134

1001 Insults, Put-Downs, and Comebacks

Also by the Author

Teaching Riding at Summer Camp
Panorama of American Horses
Civil Rights (Vols. 1 & 2)
Get a Horse!
Take Me Home
The Second-Time Single Man's Survival Handbook
Old as the Hills
Horseback Vacation Guide
Schooling to Show
The Whole Horse Catalog
Riding's a Joy
All the King's Horses
The Beautiful Baby Naming Book
Riding for a Fall
The Polo Primer
The Ultimate Fishing Guide
Caught Me a Big 'Un
The Complete Book of the American Quarter Horse
Two Bits' Book of the American Quarter Horse
Essential Riding
The Illustrated Horseman's Dictionary
The Greatest Horse Stories Ever Told
Classic Horse Stories
1001 Smartest Things Ever Said
1001 Dumbest Things Ever Said

1001 Insults, Put-Downs, and Come-Backs

Edited and with an Introduction by

Steven D. Price

THE LYONS PRESS
Guilford, Connecticut
An imprint of The Globe Pequot Press

The Lyons Press is an imprint of The Globe Pequot Press.

10 9 8 7 6 5 4 3 2 1

Printed in the United States of America

Designed by Carol Sawyer/Rose Design

ISBN 1-59228-797-2

Library of Congress Cataloging-in-Publication Data is available on file.

Contents

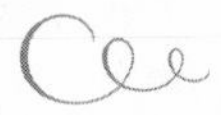

The point of quotations is that one can use another's words to be insulting.

—*Amanda Cross*

Introduction

Can you remember the first insulting remark you ever made or for that matter was made to you? I know I can't (although "you big doody-head" might well have figured prominently). That's because almost as soon as we learn to speak, we learn to speak ill of someone. We improve with age, opportunity, and practice until, at least for those of us who choose to do so, our ability to pitch verbal vitriol becomes honed to a fine point.

Why do we insult? At the most basic level, it's oral warfare, a way to attack or defend without literally drawing blood. It's also a way to relieve our anger, or in the words of Mark Twain, "In certain trying circumstances, urgent circumstances, desperate circumstances, profanity furnishes a relief denied often to prayer."

At the least imaginative level are those four-letter references to excretory and reproductive functions hurled during bouts of road rage or on uncensored "shock jock" radio. You know the kind—put most delicately, as Woody Allen did, "Some guy hit my fender, and I told him 'be fruitful, and multiply.' But not in those words."

If four-letter word curses are sledge hammers, far more inventive and possibly far more damaging are the stilettos of subtlety, such as when a noted bore told James McNeill Whistler that he passed by his house the previous evening, to which Whistler replied—with a sweet smile—"thank you."

Not all insulting is done in anger. Idle teenage hours have been spent hanging out with friends and engaging in duels known variously as "rank fights," "capping," "joaning," or "the dozens." Although my pals and I teased and traded abuse about each other's physical appearance, girlfriends' attributes, and other items of immediacy and interest, we pulled punches where appropriate. To get the better of your opponent was the goal, but we took care not to traumatize fragile adolescent psyches in the process. (A variation of "the dozens" remains popular, at least in certain quarters. That would be the fine art of dissing—short for "disrespecting"—someone's mother. This is dangerous ground to tread because in many cultures one's mother is elevated to the level of the Madonna—not the salacious singer, of course). The genre is better known as "Yo' Mama," of which this book contains some of the more imaginative examples.

Most imaginative of all are what might be lumped under the heading "snappy comebacks," those rejoinders that happen without the speaker missing a beat. Wit is essential, such as when Clare Booth Luce stepped aside to let Dorothy Parker pass ahead through a doorway, simpering "Age before beauty" and Parker swept by her, replying "Pearls before swine." Or when President Calvin Coolidge, who was noted for his miserly approach to speech, was told "Mr. President, I bet my friend that I could get you to say three words to me" and replied, "You lose."

Not everyone, however, is blessed with the mental dexterity to come up with an instant rejoinder, and how many times have we thought of a devastating response, but well after the fact. The French call this *l'esprit de l'escalier*, which translates as "the wit of the staircase," the line that comes to you as you're walking downstairs.

Snappy retorts that have a time lag also qualify, or else we'd miss out on such gems as when right before a Christmas vacation Yale literature professor William Lyons Phelps marked an examination paper on which was written "God only knows the answer to this question. Merry Christmas" with "God gets an A. You get an F. Happy New Year." Or when George Bernard Shaw sent Winston Churchill two tickets for the first night of one of his plays with a note saying: "Bring a friend—if you have one," and Churchill, returning the tickets and writing that he would not be able to attend but "I would be grateful for tickets for the second night—if there is one."

Cobbling this book together, I was struck by the intensity of dislike that musicians, and especially composers, have had for each other. Take for example, Chopin on Berlioz: "Berlioz composes by splashing his pen over the manuscript and leaving the issue to chance" and Tchaikovsky's pithy and pungent view of Brahms: "What a giftless bastard!" Nor did it matter that they were not were contemporaries who had axes to grind, as in Berlioz's assessment of Handel: "A tub of pork and beer."

The same applies to writers. Said poet James Dickey, "If it were thought that anything I wrote was influenced by Robert Frost, I would take that particular piece of mine, shred it, and flush it down the toilet, hoping not to clog the pipes." "He had a mind so fine that no idea could violate it," was T. S. Eliot's view of Henry James, while Mark Twain's assessment of James Fenimore Cooper was an equally acerbic, "Now I feel sure, deep down in my heart, that Cooper wrote about the poorest English that exists in our language, and that the English of [The] *Deerslayer* is the very worst that even Cooper ever wrote."

William Shakespeare deserves a section to himself, and he gets one here. Almost all of his plays contain insults, from the well-known (Hamlet on Rosencrantz and Guildenstern: "My two schoolfellows. Whom I shall trust as I will adders' fangs") and the typically Falstaffian ("Why, thou clay brained guts, thou knotty pated fool, thou whoreson obscene greasy tallow catch") to the more obscure but equally cutting as in Troilus and Cressida's "He has not so much a brain as ear-wax."

Countries come in for their fair share of lambasting. The United States is the butt of many insults, such as Georges Clemenceau's "America is the only nation in history which has miraculously gone directly from barbarism to degeneration without the usual interval of civilization." Other nations get theirs, too, however, as in the German aphorism that "The friendship of the French is like their wine, exquisite, but of short duration" and the Greek warning that "If a Russian is in the hills, count your olives."

Politics and history have provided any number of nuggets. When Prime Minister Benjamin Disraeli was asked to distinguish between a misfortune and a calamity, he replied that if his political opponent William Gladstone "fell into the Thames, that would be a misfortune; if someone pulled him out, that would be a calamity." Or Ralph Waldo Emerson's view of Daniel Webster: "The word liberty in the mouth of Mr. Webster sounds like the word love in the mouth of a courtesan."

The presidency has been such a fertile field that it receives its own section. As examples, Harry S. Truman felt about Richard Nixon that "He can lie out of both sides of his mouth at the same time, and if he ever caught himself telling the truth, he'd lie just to keep his hand in," while "He is a bewildered, confounded, and miserably perplexed man" is how Abraham Lincoln described James Polk.

From the field of sports comes a score of Hall of Famers. When Joe Frazier suggested that Muhammad Ali "is phony, using his blackness to get his way," The Greatest shot back that "Joe Frazier is so ugly, he should donate his face to the U.S. Bureau of Wildlife." Somewhat more circumspect was the anonymous radio commentator who announced that the Chicago Cubs "were taking batting practice, and the pitching machine threw a no-hitter."

Show business—movies, television, theater—has putdowns galore. Tony Curtis described his love scene with *Some Like It Hot* costar Marilyn Monroe as "It's like kissing Hitler." Richard Harris assessed a fellow actor with "Michael Caine compares himself to Gene Hackman. This is foolish. Mr. Caine is about as dangerous as Laurel and Hardy, or indeed both, and as intimidating as Shirley Temple." Red Skelton took a look at the crowd that attended the funeral of Harry Cohn, the widely feared and disliked head of Columbia Pictures, and said, "It proves what they always say: give the public what they want to see, and they'll come out for it."

One relevant show biz subspecialty is "insult" comedy. Among that genre's foremost practitioners is Don Rickles, whose career took off because of a line that this book quotes and that deserves a bit of background. In 1957, Frank Sinatra wandered into a small Hollywood nightclub where Rickles, then an "unknown," was performing. Rickles spotted Sinatra and told him, "I just saw your movie *The Pride and the Passion* and I want to tell you, the cannon's acting was great." Followed up by "Make yourself at home, Frank. Hit somebody." The audience turned to see how Sinatra would respond, and when he burst out laughing, the remark brought down the house—and Rickles' career was made.

Insult comedians are on stage and television, and "shock jocks" are on the radio, as are rap singers who spew their anti-just-about-everything venom. Trash-talking sports figures are widely quoted. Four-letter words are routinely heard in public. No wonder that our culture has been called dumbed-down, coarse, or worse. Some segments of society don't care, while others do, but for better or worse, that's who we are and what we've become. Gone are the days of Thumper's advice to Bambi that "if you can't say anything nice, don't say anything at all"—if indeed, as this book amply demonstrates, any generation in history could have passed that rabbit test.

Finally, and by way of acknowledgment, when the definitive history of insults, putdowns, and comebacks is written, the contributions made by Rich Goldman, Fred Sagarin, Hank Roth, and other gentlemen rankers of the Camp Taconic waiters' tent will be more than a footnote.

Special thanks go to my editor, Lisa Purcell, and to Abby Michaels for her interest in this project.

STEVEN D. PRICE
NEW YORK, NEW YORK
JUNE 2005

I.

Literary Insults

Throwing The Book

Ouch.

—*Alexander Woollcott, his entire review of a play entitled* Wham!

Thank you for sending me a copy of your book; I'll waste no time reading it.

—*Moses Hadas*

An editor should have a pimp for a brother so he'd have someone to look up to.

—*Gene Fowler*

From the moment I picked your book up until I laid it down I was convulsed with laughter. Some day I intend reading it.

—*Groucho Marx*

Fine words! I wonder where you stole them.

—*Jonathan Swift*

Nature, not content with denying him the ability to think, has endowed him with the ability to write.

—*A. E. Housman on an unidentified author*

I am returning this otherwise good typing paper to you because someone has printed gibberish all over it and put your name at the top.

—*anonymous English professor, Ohio University*

I am sitting in the smallest room of my house. I have your review before me. In a moment it will be behind me!

—*composer Max Reger to Rudolph Louis, music critic of a Munich newspaper*

This is not a book that should be tossed lightly aside. It should be hurled with great force.

—*Dorothy Parker, reviewing* The Cardinal's Mistress, *a novel by Benito Mussolini*

This is one of those big, fat paperbacks, intended to while away a monsoon or two, which, if thrown with a good over-arm action, will bring a water buffalo to its knees.

—*Nancy Banks-Smith, review of M. M. Kaye's* The Far Pavilions

Gibbon is an ugly, affected, disgusting fellow and poisons our literary club for me. I class him among infidel wasps and venomous insects.

—*James Boswell on Edward Gibbon, author of* The Decline and Fall of the Roman Empire

Gibbon's style is detestable; but it is not the worst thing about him.

—*Samuel Taylor Coleridge on Edward Gibbon*

Always willing to lend a helping hand to the one above him.

—F. Scott Fitzgerald on Ernest Hemingway

I have more to say than Hemingway, and God knows, I say it better than Faulkner.

—Carson McCullers

He has never been known to use a word that might send a reader to the dictionary.

—William Faulkner on Ernest Hemingway

Poor Faulkner. Does he really think big emotions come from big words?

—Ernest Hemingway on William Faulkner

He uses a lot of big words, and his sentences are from here to the airport.

—*Carolyn Chute on William Faulkner*

Even those who call Mr. Faulkner our greatest literary sadist do not fully appreciate him, for it is not merely his characters who have to run the gauntlet but also his readers.

—*Clifton Fadiman on William Faulkner*

He was a great friend of mine. Well, as much as you could be a friend of his, unless you were a fourteen-year-old nymphet.

—*Truman Capote on William Faulkner*

That's not writing, that's typewriting.

—*Truman Capote on Jack Kerouac*

A great zircon in the diadem of American literature.

—*Gore Vidal on Truman Capote*

A fungus of pendulous shape.

—*Alice James on George Eliot, pseudonym of Mary Ann Evans*

George Eliot has the heart of Sappho; but the face, with the long proboscis, the protruding teeth of the Apocalyptic horse, betrayed animality.

—George Meredith on George Eliot

If it were thought that anything I wrote was influenced by Robert Frost, I would take that particular piece of mine, shred it, and flush it down the toilet, hoping not to clog the pipes.

—James Dickey on Robert Frost

A nice, acrid, savage, pathetic old chap.

—I. A. Richards on Robert Frost

T. S. Eliot and I like to play, but I like to play euchre, while he likes to play Eucharist.

—Robert Frost on T. S. Eliot

She preserved to the age of fifty-six that contempt for ideas which is normal among boys and girls of fifteen.

—Odell Shepherd on Louisa May Alcott

Every word she writes is a lie, including "and" and "the."

—Mary McCarthy on Lillian Hellman

Writers are interesting people, but often mean and petty.

—Lillian Hellman

She bellies up to the gourmet cracker-barrel and delivers laid-back wisdom with the serenity of a down-home Buddha who has discovered that stool softeners really work.

—Florence King on Molly Ivins

The affair between Margot Asquith and Margot Asquith will live as one of the prettiest love stories in all literature.

—Dorothy Parker

To those she did not like . . . she was a stiletto made of sugar.

—John Mason Brown on Dorothy Parker

That insolent little ruffian, that crapulous lout. When he quitted a sofa, he left behind him a smear.

—*Norman Cameron on Dylan Thomas*

Isn't she a poisonous thing of a woman, lying, concealing, flipping, plagiarizing, misquoting, and being as clever a crooked literary publicist as ever.

—*Dylan Thomas on Dame Edith Sitwell*

I am fairly unrepentant about her poetry. I really think that three quarters of it is gibberish. However, I must crush down these thoughts, otherwise the dove of peace will shit on me.

—*Noel Coward on Dame Edith Sitwell*

A great many people now reading and writing would be better employed keeping rabbits.

—*Dame Edith Sitwell*

Virginia Woolf's writing is no more than glamorous knitting. I believe she must have a pattern somewhere.

—*Dame Edith Sitwell*

I am reading Henry James . . . and feel myself as one entombed in a block of smooth amber.

—*Virginia Woolf on Henry James*

Henry James was one of the nicest old ladies I ever met.

—*William Faulkner*

I have just read a long novel by Henry James. Much of it made me think of the priest condemned for a long space to confess nuns.

—*William Butler Yeats on Henry James*

. . . looking himself in his old cloak like a huge umbrella left behind by some picnic party.

—*George Moore on William Butler Yeats*

He had a mind so fine that no idea could violate it.

—*T. S. Eliot on Henry James*

A little emasculated mass of inanity.

—*Theodore Roosevelt on Henry James*

He spares no resource in telling of his dead inventions. . . . Bare verbs he rarely tolerates. He splits infinitives and fills them up with adverbial stuffing. He presses the passing colloquialism into his service. His vast paragraphs sweat and struggle; they could not sweat and elbow and struggle more if God Himself was the processional meaning to which they sought to come.

—*H. G. Wells on Henry James*

I doubt that the infant monster has any more to give.

—Henry James on Rudyard Kipling

A jingo imperialist, morally insensitive and aesthetically disgusting.

—George Orwell on Rudyard Kipling

He would not blow his nose without moralizing on conditions in the handkerchief industry.

—Cyril Connolly on George Orwell

He's a full-fledged housewife from Kansas with all the prejudices.

—*Gore Vidal on Truman Capote*

In her last days, she resembled a spoiled pear.

—*Gore Vidal on Gertrude Stein*

She was a master at making nothing happen very slowly.

—*Clifton Fadiman on Gertrude Stein*

. . . the jingle man.

—*Ralph Waldo Emerson on Edgar Allan Poe*

Poe's prose is unreadable, like Jane Austen's.

—*Mark Twain on Edgar Allan Poe*

Just the omission of Jane Austen's books alone would make a fairly good library out of a library that hadn't a book in it.

—*Mark Twain*

A hack writer who would have been considered fourth rate in Europe, who tried out a few of the old proven "sure-fire" literary skeletons with sufficient local color to intrigue the superficial and the lazy.

—*William Faulkner on Mark Twain*

A hoary-headed and toothless baboon.

—Thomas Carlyle on Ralph Waldo Emerson

. . . repeating himself, shampooing himself, [as if] Christ himself.

—Henry David Thoreau on Ralph Waldo Emerson

I love Henry, but I cannot like him; and as for taking his arm, I should as soon think of taking the arm of an elm-tree.

—unnamed friend of Henry David Thoreau

The stupid person's idea of a clever person.

—Elizabeth Bowen on Aldous Huxley

Jeffery Archer is proof of the proposition that in each of us lurks a bad novel.

—Julian Critchley

His style has the desperate jauntiness of an orchestra fiddling away for dear life on a sinking ship.

—Edmund Wilson on Evelyn Waugh

The cruelest thing that has happened to Lincoln since he was shot by Booth has been to fall into the hands of Carl Sandburg.

—*Edmund Wilson*

He writes as if he had a loose upper plate . . . [and his] careful and pedestrian and sometimes rather clever book reviews misguide one into thinking there is something in his head besides mucilage.

—*Raymond Chandler on Edmund Wilson.*

He is the sort of man who could spend a year in flophouses, researching flophouses, and write a play about flophouses that would be no more real than a play by a man who had never been in a flophouse, but had only read about them.

—*Raymond Chandler on Eugene O'Neill*

Everything he touches smells like a billygoat. He is every kind of a writer I detest, a faux naif, a Proust in greasy overalls.

—*Raymond Chandler on James M. Cain*

Reading Joseph Conrad is like gargling with broken glass.

—*Hugh Leonard*

A man who so much resembled a Baked Alaska—sweet, warm and gungy on the outside, hard and cold within.

—*Joseph O'Connor on C. P. Snow*

An agile but unintelligent and abnormal German, possessed of the mania of grandeur.

—Leo Tolstoy on Friedrich Wilhelm Nietzsche

The triumph of sugar over diabetes.

—George Jean Nathan on J. M. Barrie

Oscar Wilde's talent seems to me to be essentially rootless, something growing in glass on a little water.

—George Moore on Oscar Wilde

A monstrous orchid.

—Oscar Wilde on Aubrey Beardsley

One must have a heart of stone to read the death of little Nell without laughing.

—Oscar Wilde on Charles Dickens' Little Dorrit

There are two ways of disliking poetry. One way is to dislike it; the other is to read [Alexander] Pope.

—Oscar Wilde

[George] Meredith is a prose Browning—and so is Browning.

—*Oscar Wilde*

He hasn't an enemy in the world, and none of his friends like him.

—*Oscar Wilde on George Bernard Shaw*

I remember coming across him at the Grand Canyon and finding him peevish, refusing to admire it or even look at it properly. He was jealous of it.

—*J. B. Priestley on George Bernard Shaw*

A freakish homunculus germinated outside lawful procreation.

—Henry Arthur Jones on George Bernard Shaw

He writes like a Pakistani who had learned English when he was twelve years old in order to become a chartered accountant.

—John Osborne on George Bernard Shaw

He writes his plays for the ages—the ages between five and twelve.

—George Jean Nathan on George Bernard Shaw

Concerning no subject would Shaw be deterred by the minor accident of total ignorance from penning a definitive opinion.

—*Roger Scruton on George Bernard Shaw*

The reading of *Dawn* is a strain upon many parts, but the worst wear and tear fall on the forearms. After holding the massive volume for the half-day necessary to its perusal (well, look at that, would you? "massive volume" and "perusal," one right after the other! You see how contagious Mr. D.'s manner is?), my arms ached with a slow, mean persistence beyond the services of aspirin or of liniment. . . . And I can't truly feel that *Dawn* was worth it. If I must have aches, I had rather gain them in the first tennis of the season, and get my back into it.

—*Dorothy Parker on Theodore Dreiser*

Theodore Dreiser
Should ought to write nicer.

—*Dorothy Parker*

A huge pendulum attached to a small clock.

—*Ivan Panin on Samuel Taylor Coleridge*

A fat little flabby person, with the face of a baker, the clothes of a cobbler, the size of a barrel maker, the manners of a stocking salesman, and the dress of an innkeeper.

—*Victor de Balabin on Honoré de Balzac*

An enchanting toad of a man.

—Helen Hayes on Robert Benchley

His imagination resembles the wings of an ostrich.

—Thomas Babington Macaulay on John Dryden

An animated adenoid.

—Norman Douglas on Ford Madox Ford

He was humane but not human.

—e e cummings on Ezra Pound

To me Pound remains the exquisite showman without the show.

—*Ben Hecht on Ezra Pound*

He is able to turn an unplotted, unworkable manuscript into an unplotted and unworkable manuscript with a lot of sex.

—*Tom Volpe on Harold Robbins*

Yes it was very good of God to let Carlyle and Mrs. Carlyle marry one another and so make only two people miserable instead of four, besides being very amusing.

—*Samuel Butler on Thomas Carlyle and his wife*

Sitting in a sewer and adding to it.

—Thomas Carlyle on Algernon Charles Swinburne

Charles Lamb I sincerely believe to be in some considerable degree insane. A more pitiful, ricketty, gasping, staggering, stammering Tom fool I do not know. He is witty by denying truisms, and abjuring good manners. His speech wriggles hither and thither with an incessant painful fluctuation; not an opinion in it or a fact or even a phrase that you can thank him for: more like a convulsion fit than natural systole and diastole.—Besides he is now a confirmed shameless drunkard: asks vehemently for gin-and-water in strangers' houses; tipples until he is utterly mad, and is only not thrown out of doors because he is too much despised for taking such trouble with him. Poor Lamb! Poor England where such a despicable abortion is named genius!

—Thomas Carlyle on Charles Lamb

An abortion of George Sand.

—George Moore on Thomas Hardy

A great cow full of ink.

—Gustave Flaubert on George Sand

A dirty man with opium-glazed eyes and rat-taily hair.

—Lady Frederick Cavendish on Alfred, Lord Tennyson

Reading him is like wading through glue.

—Alfred, Lord Tennyson on Ben Johnson

A tall, thin, spectacled man with the face of a harassed rat.

—Russell Maloney on James Thurber

A large shaggy dog unchained scouring the beaches of the world and baying at the moon.

—Robert Louis Stevenson on Walt Whitman

Dank, limber verses, stuft with lakeside sedges
And propt with rotten stakes from rotten hedges.

—Walter Savage Landor on William Wordsworth

I wish I was as cocksure of anything as Tom Macaulay is of everything.

—Lord Melbourne on Thomas Babington Macaulay

Sir, you have but two subjects, yourself and me. I am sick of both.

—Samuel Johnson when James Boswell was cross-examining a third person about him in his presence

Nay, sir, we'll send you to him. If your presence doesn't drive a man out of his house, nothing will.

—Samuel Johnson to James Boswell, discussing how to get a friend to leave London

None ever wished it longer.

—*Samuel Johnson on John Milton's* Paradise Lost

. . . that fellow Richardson, on the contrary, could not be contented to sail quietly down the stream of reputation, without longing to taste the froth from every stroke of the oar.

—*Samuel Johnson on Samuel Richardson*

Sir, he was dull in company, dull in his closet, dull everywhere. He was dull in a new way, and that made many people think him great. He was a mechanical poet.

—*Samuel Johnson on Thomas Gray*

He walked as if he had fouled his small clothes and looks as if he smelt it.

—*Christopher Smart on Thomas Gray*

It is amazing how little Goldsmith knows. He seldom comes where he is not more ignorant than any one else.

—*Samuel Johnson on Oliver Goldsmith*

There is no arguing with Johnson; for when his pistol misses fire, he knocks you down with the butt end of it.

—*Oliver Goldsmith on Samuel Johnson*

Mad, bad, and dangerous to know.

—*Lady Caroline Lamb on Lord Byron*

The world is rid of him, but the deadly slime of his touch remains.

—*John Constable on Lord Byron*

Mr. Lawrence looked like a plaster gnome on a stone toadstool in some suburban garden . . . he looked as if he had just returned from spending an uncomfortable night in a very dark cave.

—*Dame Edith Sitwell on D. H. Lawrence*

Nothing but old fags and cabbage-stumps of quotations from the Bible and the rest, stewed in the juice of deliberate, journalistic dirty-mindedness.

—*D. H. Lawrence on James Joyce*

the work of a queasy undergraduate squeezing his pimples.

—*Virginia Woolf on James Joyce's* Ulysses

With a pig's eyes that never look up, with a pig's snout that loves muck, with a pig's brain that knows only the sty, and with a pig's squeal that cries only when he is hurt, he sometimes opens his pig's mouth, tusked and ugly, and lets out the voice of God, railing at the whitewash that covers the manure about his habitat.

—*William Allen White on H. L. Mencken*

Mr. Mencken's prose sounds like large stones being thrown into a dumpcart.

—*Robert Littell*

Author to William Dean Howells: "I don't seem to write as well as I used to."

Howells: "Oh, yes you do. You write as well as ever you did. But your taste has improved."

Nay, in his stile and writing there is the same mixture of vicious contrarieties;—the most groveling ideas are conveyed in the most inflated language; giving mock consequence to low cavils, and uttering quibbles in heroics; so that his compositions disgust the mind's taste, as much as his actions excite the soul's abhorrence.

—*Richard Brinsley Sheridan on Warren Hastings, governor general of India*

I am His Highness's dog at Kew;
Pray tell me, Sir, whose dog are you?

—*inscription on a dog collar presented by Alexander Pope to the Prince of Wales*

Mr. Fitzgerald is a novelist and Mrs. Fitzgerald is a novelty.

—*Ring Lardner on F. Scott and Zelda Fitzgerald*

In fact, Mr. Fitzgerald—I believe that is how he spells his name—seems to believe that plagiarism begins at home.

—*Zelda Fitzgerald on F. Scott Fitzgerald's* The Beautiful and the Damned *(she felt that the book was more than autobiographical, but taken from her diaries)*

ON JOURNALISTS AND JOURNALISM

Your connection with any newspaper would be a disgrace and degradation. I would rather sell gin to poor people and poison them that way.

—Sir Walter Scott to a journalist friend

The lowest depth to which people can sink before God is defined by the word "journalist." If I were a father and had a daughter who was seduced I should despair over her; I would hope for her salvation. But if I had a son who became a journalist and continued to be one for five years, I would give him up.

—Søren Kierkegaard

The only qualities for real success in journalism are ratlike cunning, a plausible manner and a little literary ability.

—Nicholas Tomalin

If a person is not talented enough to be a novelist, not smart enough to be a lawyer, and his hands are too shaky to perform operations, he becomes a journalist.

—*Norman Mailer*

A journalist is a person who works harder than any other lazy person in the world.

—*Anonymous*

The fact that a man is a newspaper reporter is evidence of some flaw of character.

—*Lyndon B. Johnson*

Archibald Forbes rarely waited for the end of a battle to report it and sometimes did not even wait for the beginning.

—*R. J. Cruickshank, editor of the* Daily News, *describing Forbes, the paper's famous war correspondent of the 1870s and 1880s*

I believe in equality for everyone, except reporters and photographers.

—*Mohandas Gandhi*

In the United States today, we have more than our share of the nattering nabobs of negativism. They have formed their own 4-H Club—the hopeless, hysterical hypochondriacs of history.

—*Spiro T. Agnew, referring to the media*

From literature

How There Arose between the Cake-Peddlers of Lerne and Gargantua's Countrymen the Great Quarrel from Which Huge Wars Were to Spring

The cake-peddlers were by no means inclined to grant the shepherd's request, but (what was worse) proceeded to insult the latter terribly, calling them "scum of the earth, toothless bastards, red-headed rogues, chippy-chasers, filthy wretches of the kind that dung in the bed, big lubbers, sneaky curs, lazy hounds, pretty boys, pot-bellies, windjammers, good-for-nothings, clodhoppers, bad customers, greedy beggars, blowhards, mamma's darlings, monkey-faces, loafers, bums, big boobs, scoundrels, simpletons, silly jokers, dudes, teeth-chattering tramps, dirty cowherds, and dung-dripping shepherds," with other defamatory epithets, adding that it was not for the likes of them to be eating these fine cakes, but that they ought to be satisfied with coarse, lumpy bread and big round loaves.

—*François Rabelais,* Gargantua (1534)

And in conclusion, Edmond Rostand's Cyrano de Bergerac teaches a young nobleman the fine art of insulting as he rattles off nineteen far more clever things the youngster might have said and delivers a few zingers of his own:

The Viscount: But wait! I'll treat him to . . . one of my quips! . . . See here! . . . (He goes up to Cyrano, who is watching him, and with a conceited air): Sir, your nose is . . . hmm . . . it is . . . very big!

Cyrano: (gravely): Very!

The Viscount: (laughing): Ha!

Cyrano: (imperturbably): Is that all? . . .

The Viscount: What do you mean?

Cyrano: Ah no! young blade! That was a trifle short! You might have said at least a hundred things by varying the tone . . . like this, suppose, . . . Aggressive: "Sir, if I had such a nose I'd amputate it!" Friendly: "When you sup it must annoy you, dipping in your cup; You need a drinking-bowl of special shape!" Descriptive: "'Tis a rock! . . . a peak! . . . a cape!—A cape, forsooth! 'Tis a peninsular!" Curious: "How serves that oblong capsular? For scissor-sheath? Or pot to hold your ink?" Gracious: "You love the little birds, I think? I see you've managed with a fond research to find their tiny claws a roomy perch!" Truculent: "When you smoke your pipe . . . suppose that the tobacco-smoke spouts from your nose—Do not the neighbors, as the fumes rise higher, cry terror-struck: 'The chimney is afire'?" Considerate: "Take care, . . . your head bowed low by such a weight . . . lest head o'er heels you go!" Tender: "Pray get a small umbrella made, lest its bright color in the sun should fade!" Pedantic: "That beast Aristophanes names Hippocamelelephantoles Must have possessed just such a solid lump of flesh and bone, beneath his forehead's bump!" Cavalier: "The last fashion, friend, that hook? To hang your hat on? 'Tis a useful crook!" Emphatic: "No wind, O majestic nose, can give THEE cold!—save when the mistral blows!" Dramatic: "When it bleeds, what a Red Sea!" Admiring: "Sign for a perfumery!" Lyric: "Is this a conch? . . . a Triton you?" Simple: "When is the monument on view?" Rustic: "That thing a nose? Marry-come-up! 'Tis a dwarf pumpkin, or a prize turnip!" Military: "Point against cavalry!" Practical: "Put it in a lottery! Assuredly 'twould be the biggest prize!" Or . . . parodying Pyramus' sighs . . ."Behold the nose that mars the harmony of its master's phiz! blushing its treachery!"—Such, my dear sir, is what you might have said, Had you of wit or letters the least jot: But, O most lamentable man!—of wit you never had an atom and of letters you have three letters only!—they spell Ass!

II.

SHOW BUSINESS

Roasting the Hams

Don Rickles

Let's begin with Mister Warmth himself:

Frank, just make yourself at home and hit somebody.
—*to Frank Sinatra*

Who picks your clothes, Stevie Wonder?
—*to David Letterman*

What are you doing here? Is the war over?
—*to Bob Hope*

Ricardo is here tonight. Here's some mud—finish your hut!
—*to Ricardo Montalban*

A glass of milk, huh, Pat? I hope you get prickly heat all over your stomach!

—*to Pat Boone*

And this exchange with Dean Martin:

Rickles: It takes many years to become a great comedian . . .

Martin: Yeah, and you ain't reached that year yet!

Rickles [alluding to Martin's former partner, Jerry Lewis, with whom he was feuding]: Ah, thanks, Jerry!

Henny Youngman

The king of the one-liners could always be counted on for a zinger.

If you have your life to live over again, don't do it.

If you had your life to live over again, do it overseas.

He was born on April 2. A day late.

I'd like to say we're glad you're here—I'd like to say it, but . . .

I'm paid to make an idiot out of myself. Why do you do it for free?

Was that suit made to order? Where were you at the time?

You have the Midas touch. Everything you touch turns to a muffler.

You have a ready wit. Tell me when it's ready.

You look like a talent scout for a cemetery.

The more I think of you, the less I think of you.

RODNEY DANGERFIELD

Knew how to focus his humor on himself.

My psychiatrist told me I'm going crazy. I said, "If you don't mind, I'd like a second opinion." He says, "All right—you're ugly too!"

I'm not a sexy guy. I went to a hooker. I dropped my pants. She dropped her price.

What a childhood I had, why, when I took my first step, my old man tripped me!

I tell ya when I was a kid, all I knew was rejection. My yo-yo, it never came back!

I worked in a pet store and people kept asking how big I'd get.

GROUCHO MARX

A past master of the put-down, whether on the screen or in real life.

I've had a perfectly wonderful evening. But this wasn't it.

You've got the brain of a four year old boy; and I bet he was glad to get rid of it.

Why don't you bore a hole in yourself and let the sap run out?

I married your mother because I wanted children, imagine my disappointment when you came along.

Remember men, we're fighting for this woman's honor; which is probably more than she ever did.

Don't look now, but there's one too many in this room and I think it's you.

He may look like an idiot and talk like an idiot but don't let that fool you. He really is an idiot.

I never forget a face, but in your case I'll make an exception.

I didn't like the play, but then I saw it under adverse conditions—the curtain was up.

And from his brother Harpo:

[Alexander Woollcott] looked like something that had gotten loose from Macy's Thanksgiving Day Parade.

If there's anything disgusting about the movie business, it's the whoredom of my peers.

—*Sean Penn*

You can pick out actors by the glazed look that comes into their eyes when the conversation wanders away from themselves.

—*Michael Wilding*

I never said all actors are cattle; what I said was all actors should be treated like cattle.

—*Alfred Hitchcock*

Modesty is the artifice of actors, similar to passion in call girls.

—*attributed to Jackie Gleason*

[Liberace] is the summit of sex—the pinnacle of masculine, feminine, and neuter. Everything that he, she, and it can ever want.

I spoke to sad but kindly men on this newspaper who have met every celebrity coming from America for the past thirty years. They say that this deadly, winking, sniggering, snuggling, chromium-plated, scent-impregnated, luminous, quivering, giggling, fruit-flavored, mincing, ice-covered heap of mother love has had the biggest reception and impact on London since Charlie Chaplin arrived at the same station, Waterloo, on September 12, 1921 . . .

He reeks with emetic language that can only make grown men long for a quiet corner, an aspidistra, a handkerchief, and the old heave-ho. Without doubt, he is the biggest sentimental vomit of all time. Slobbering over his mother, winking at his brother, and counting the cash at every second, this superb piece of calculating candy-floss has an answer for every situation.

There must be something wrong with us that our teenagers longing for sex and our middle-aged matrons fed up with sex alike should fall for such a sugary mountain of jingling claptrap wrapped up in such a preposterous clown.

—*English* Daily Mirror *columnist William Connor, writing under the pen name "Cassandra." (Following his successful libel trial against the* Mirror, *Liberace came out with his celebrated remark, "I cried all the way to the bank!")*

He is to acting what Liberace was to pumping iron.

—Rex Reed on Sylvester Stallone

It proves what they always say: give the public what they want to see, and they'll come out for it.

—Red Skelton on the funeral of Harry Cohn, much-feared longtime head of Columbia Pictures

The biggest bug in the manure pile.

—Elia Kazan on Harry Cohn

Work hard. Save your money. When you have enough money saved, buy an axe. Use it to chop off your head and stop bothering me.

—Lionel Barrymore to an aspiring actor asking for advice

He was the most boring drunk in the history of the theater.

—*Ben Gazzara on Jason Robards*

When he has a party, you not only bring your own scotch, you bring your own rocks.

—*George Burns on Jack Benny*

He's done everybody's act. He's a parrot with skin on.

—*Fred Allen on Milton Berle*

He's an anesthetist—Prince Valium.

—*Mort Sahl on Johnny Carson*

A great actress, from the waist down.

—Dame Margaret Kendal on Sarah Bernhardt

She ran the whole gamut of emotions from A to B.

—Dorothy Parker on a Katharine Hepburn performance

Acting is the most minor of gifts and not a very high-class way to earn a living. After all, Shirley Temple could do it at the age of four.

—Katharine Hepburn

Michael Caine compares himself to Gene Hackman. This is foolish. Hackman is an intimidating and dangerous actor. Mr. Caine is about as dangerous as Laurel and Hardy, or indeed both, and as intimidating as Shirley Temple.

—Richard Harris

A day away from Tallulah is like a month in the country.

—Howard Dietz on temperamental actress Tallulah Bankhead

Most of the time he sounds like he has a mouth full of toilet paper.

—Rex Reed on Marlon Brando

She looks like something that would eat its young.

—Dorothy Parker on British actress Dame Edith Evans

She was divinely, hysterically, insanely malevolent.

—*Bette Davis on the silent movie star Theda Bara*

I wonder if the trend in making [movies about] maids who don't speak English [as] heroines is related to the trend of guys who like to watch Kelly Ripa in the morning with the sound turned off?

—*Maureen Dowd*

She must use Novocain lipstick.

—*Jack Paar on newspaper columnist and deadpan TV panelist Dorothy Kilgallen*

She speaks five languages and can't act in any of them.

—*Sir John Gielgud on Ingrid Bergman*

Her hair lounges on her shoulders like an anesthetized cocker spaniel.

—Henry Allen on Lauren Bacall

His ears made him look like a taxicab with both doors open.

—Howard Hughes on Clark Gable

I have more talent in my smallest fart than you have in your entire body.

—Walter Matthau to Barbra Streisand

A cross between an aardvark and an albino rat.

—John Simon on Barbra Streisand

She has discovered the secret of perpetual middle age.
She not only worships the golden calf, she barbecues it for lunch.

—Oscar Levant on Zsa Zsa Gabor

You can calculate Zsa Zsa Gabor's age by the rings on her fingers.

—Bob Hope

She should get a divorce and settle down.

—Jack Paar on Zsa Zsa Gabor

A buxom milkmaid reminiscent of a cow wearing a girdle, and both have the same amount of acting talent.

—Mr. Blackwell on Brigitte Bardot

Her body has gone to her head.

—*Barbara Stanwyck on Marilyn Monroe*

She has breasts of granite and a mind like a Gruyere cheese.

—*Billy Wilder on Marilyn Monroe*

She was good at being inarticulately abstracted for the same reason that midgets are good at being short.

—*Clive James on Marilyn Monroe*

It's like kissing Hitler.

—*Tony Curtis on kissing Marilyn Monroe*

She's a vacuum with nipples.

—*Otto Preminger on Marilyn Monroe*

Maybe it's the hair. Maybe it's the teeth. Maybe it's the intellect. No, it's the hair.

—*Tom Shales on Farrah Fawcett*

Dramatic art in her opinion is knowing how to fill a sweater.

—*Bette Davis on Jayne Mansfield*

Miss United Dairies herself.

—*David Niven about Jayne Mansfield*

Elizabeth Taylor looks like two small boys fighting underneath a thick blanket.

—*Mr. Blackwell*

Elizabeth Taylor's so fat, she puts mayonnaise on aspirin.

—*Joan Rivers*

She has an insipid double chin, her legs are too short, and she has a slight potbelly.

—*Richard Burton on Elizabeth Taylor*

She's like an apple turnover that got crushed in a grocery bag on a hot day.

—*Camille Paglia on Drew Barrymore*

He had the compassion of an icicle and the generosity of a pawnbroker.

—S. J. Perelman on Groucho Marx

I watched *The Music Lovers*. One can't really blame Tchaikovsky for preferring boys. Anyone might become a homosexualist who had once seen Glenda Jackson naked.

—Auberon Waugh

A face unclouded by thought.

—Lillian Hellman on Norma Shearer

She looks like she combs her hair with an eggbeater.

—Louella Parsons on Joan Collins

Miss [Joan] Crawford cannot act her way out of a brown paper bag.

—*Bette Davis*

Joan always cries a lot. Her tear ducts must be close to her bladder.

—*Bette Davis on Joan Crawford*

A kind of cross between Julia Roberts and Jack Nicholson.

—*Jeremy Novick on Lolita Davidovich*

She turned down the role of Helen Keller because she couldn't remember the lines.

—*Joan Rivers on Bo Derek*

If I found her floating in my pool, I'd punish my dog.

—Joan Rivers on Yoko Ono

When it comes to acting, Joan Rivers has the range of a wart.

—reviewer Stewart Klein

A woman whose face looked as if it had been made of sugar and someone had licked it.

—George Bernard Shaw on the dancer Isadora Duncan

Age cannot wither her, nor custom stale her infinite sameness.

—David Shipman on Marlene Dietrich

The worst and most homeliest thing to hit the screens since Liza Minelli.

—John Simon on Shelley Duvall

Hah! I always knew Frank would end up in bed with a boy!

—Ava Gardner on ex-husband's Sinatra's marriage to Mia Farrow

The Russians love Brooke Shields because her eyebrows remind them of Leonid Brezhnev.

—Robin Williams

Ms. Simpson may be the last performer in America who can make Whoopi Goldberg seem like the soul of wit.

—*Frank Rich, after actress/singer Jessica Simpson, on meeting Secretary of the Interior Gale Norton, congratulated Ms. Norton for doing "a nice job decorating the White House."*

These two prove that bad taste is positively genetic!

—*Mr. Blackwell on sisters Jessica and Ashlee Simpson*

Whatever it was that this actress never had, she still hasn't got it.

—*Bosley Crowther on Loretta Young*

Roseanne Barr is a bowling ball looking for an alley.

—*Mr. Blackwell*

I treasure every moment that I do not see her.

—*Oscar Levant on Phyllis Diller*

Her virtue was that she said what she thought, her vice that what she thought didn't amount to much.

—*Peter Ustinov on Hollywood columnist Hedda Hopper*

Armed with a wiggle and a Minnie Mouse squawk, she is coarse and charmless.

—*Sheila Johnson on Madonna*

I look at my friendship with her as like having a gall stone. You deal with it, there is pain, and then you pass it. That's all I have to say about Schmadonna.

—Sandra Bernhard on Madonna

Not in this lifetime. Why? Because I'm the only one she hasn't done it to.

—Sharon Stone, when told Madonna said she wanted to kiss her

It's a new low for actresses when you have to wonder what's between her ears instead of her legs.

—Katharine Hepburn on Sharon Stone

She is so hairy, when she lifted up her arm, I thought it was Tina Turner in her armpit.

—Joan Rivers on Madonna

I didn't know her well, but after watching her in action I didn't want to know her well.

—Joan Crawford on Judy Garland

All legs and hair with a mouth that could swallow the whole stadium and the hot-dog stand.

—Laura Lee Davies on Tina Turner

A fellow with the inventiveness of Albert Einstein but with the attention span of Daffy Duck.

—Tom Shales on Robin Williams

Martin's acting is so inept that even his impersonation of a lush seems unconvincing.

—Harry Medved on Dean Martin

In barely-there bombs, she's a taste-free pain. Let's crown her the Tacky Temptress of Wisteria Lane.

—Mr. Blackwell on Nicollette Sheridan of TV's Desperate Housewives

This is one Hilton that should be closed for renovation!

—Mr. Blackwell on Paris Hilton

Spielberg isn't a filmmaker, he's a confectioner.

—Alex Cox on Steven Spielberg

I couldn't stand Janis Joplin's voice. . . . She was just a screaming little loudmouthed chick.

—Arthur Lee on Janis Joplin

A plumber's idea of Cleopatra.

—W. C. Fields on Mae West

If people don't sit at Chaplin's feet, he goes out and stands where they are sitting.

—producer Herman J. Mankiewicz

Jack Warner has oilcloth pockets so he can steal soup.

—Wilson Mizner

My dear, you're sitting on it.

—Alfred Hitchcock, replying to actress Mary Anderson's question about what he thought was her best side

She is as wholesome as a bowl of corn flakes and at least as sexy.

—Dwight Macdonald on Doris Day

And a handful of caustic reviews:

Mr. Clarke played the King all evening as though under constant fear that someone else was about to play the ace.

—*Eugene Field, referring to Creston Clarke's performance of King Lear*

A bore is starred.

—Village Voice *review of* A Star Is Born, *starring Barbra Streisand*

It is greatly to Mrs. Patrick Campbell's credit that, bad as the play was, her acting was worse. It was a masterpiece of failure.

—*George Bernard Shaw*

When you were a little boy, somebody ought to have said "hush" just once.

—*Mrs. Patrick Campbell to George Bernard Shaw*

This is a pompous, badly acted film, full of absurd anachronisms and inconsistencies.

—*Graham Greene,* The Spectator *on* The Bride of Frankenstein *(1935)*

It has dwarfs, music, Technicolor, freak characters and Judy Garland. It can't be expected to have a sense of humor as well and as for the light touch of fantasy, it weighs like a pound of fruitcake soaking wet.

—The New Republic *on* The Wizard of Oz *(1939)*

The love story that takes us from time to time into the past is horribly wooden and clichés everywhere lower the tension.

—New Statesman *on* Casablanca (*1942*)

The old master has turned out another Hitchcock-and-bull story in which the mystery is not so much who done it as who cares.

—Time *on* Vertigo (*1958*)

The Apartment is without style or taste, shifting gears between pathos and slapstick without any transition . . . What can you do, after all, in a big insurance company? And where but in Hollywood would this situation be seen as comic material? . . . To me, *The Apartment* illustrated Hollywood's lack of contact with reality.

—*Dwight Macdonald in* Esquire *on* The Apartment (*1960*)

For this is third-rate Hitchcock, a Grand Guignol drama in which the customers hang around just for the tiny thrill at the end, like a strip-tease; and one feels as one comes out, as in both these cases, that one has been had; bad taste in the mouth. I think the film is a reflection of a most unpleasant mind, a mean, sly sadistic little mind.

—*Dwight Macdonald in* Esquire *on* Psycho *(1960)*

A cheap piece of bald-faced slapstick comedy that treats the hideous depredations of that sleazy, moronic pair as though they were as full of fun and frolic as the jazz-age cut ups in Thoroughly Modern Millie. This blending of farce with brutal killings is as pointless as it is lacking in taste . . .

—*Bosley Crowther,* The New York Times *on* Bonnie and Clyde *(1967)*

The slab is never explained, leaving 2001, for all its lively visual and mechanical spectacle, a kind of space-*Spartacus* and, more pretentious still, a shaggy God story.

—*John Simon,* The New Leader *on* 2001: A Space Odyssey *(1968)*

It's a Frankenstein monster stitched together from leftover parts. It talks. It moves in fits and starts but it has no mind of its own. . . . Looking very expensive but spiritually desperate, Part II has the air of a very long, very elaborate revue sketch.

—*Vincent Canby on* The Godfather, Part II *(1974)*

III.

The United States

Pan America

America is dumb, it's like a dumb puppy that has big teeth that can bite and hurt you, aggressive. My daughter is four, my boy is one. I'd like them to see America as a toy, a broken toy. Investigate it a little, check it out, get this feeling and then get out.

—Johnny Depp

There is a Providence that protects idiots, drunkards, children, and the United States of America.

—Otto von Bismarck

I found there a country with thirty-two religions and only one sauce.

—Charles-Maurice de Talleyrand-Perigord

Their demeanor is invariably morose, sullen, clownish and repulsive. I should think there is not, on the face of the earth, a people so entirely destitute of humor, vivacity, or the capacity for enjoyment.

—*Charles Dickens*

America is the only nation in history which has miraculously gone directly from barbarism to degeneration without the usual interval of civilization.

—*Georges Clemenceau*

No one ever went broke underestimating the taste of the great American public.

—*H. L. Mencken*

Never criticize Americans. They have the best taste that money can buy.

—*Miles Kingston*

America is a large, friendly dog in a very small room. Every time it wags its tail, it knocks over a chair.

—*Arnold Toynbee*

America knows nothing of food, love, or art.

—*Isadora Duncan*

The 100 percent American is 99 percent idiot.

—*George Bernard Shaw*

I am willing to love all mankind, except an American.

—*Samuel Johnson*

Americans are possibly the dumbest people on the planet. . . . We Americans suffer from an enforced ignorance. We don't know about anything that's happening outside our country. Our stupidity is embarrassing.

—*Michael Moore*

Americans can eat garbage, provided you sprinkle it liberally with ketchup, mustard, chili sauce, Tabasco sauce, cayenne pepper, or any other condiment which destroys the original flavor of the dish.

—*Henry Miller*

No one can be as calculatedly rude as the British, which amazes Americans, who do not understand studied insult and can only offer abuse as a substitute.

—Paul Gallico

Sir, they are a race of convicts and ought to be grateful for anything we allow them short of hanging.

—Samuel Johnson on Americans

Frustrate a Frenchman, he will drink himself to death; an Irishman, he will die of angry hypertension; a Dane, he will shoot himself; an American, he will get drunk, shoot you, then establish a million dollar aid program for your relatives. Then he will die of an ulcer.

—Samuel A. Rudin

America . . . just a nation of two hundred million used-car salesmen with all the money we need to buy guns and no qualms about killing anybody else in the world who tries to make us uncomfortable.

—*Hunter S. Thompson*

America is a mistake, a giant mistake.

—*Sigmund Freud*

Americans always try to do the right thing after they've tried everything else.

—*Winston Churchill*

America is a melting pot, the people at the bottom get burned while all the scum floats to the top.

—*Charlie King*

When good Americans die, they go to Paris. When bad Americans die, they go to America.

—*Oscar Wilde*

America . . . where laws and customs alike are based on the dreams of spinsters.

—*Bertrand Russell*

The Americans, like the English, probably make love worse than any other race.

—*Walt Whitman*

Half of the American people have never read a newspaper. Half never voted for President. One hopes it is the same half.

—*Gore Vidal*

It is absurd to say that there are neither ruins nor curiosities in America when they have their mothers and their manners.

—*Oscar Wilde*

If you're going to America, bring your own food.

—*Fran Lebowitz*

Of course, America had often been discovered before Columbus, but it had always been hushed up.

—Oscar Wilde

I love Americans, but not when they try to talk French. What a blessing it is that they never try to talk English.

—Saki (H. H. Munro)

The American male doesn't mature until he has exhausted all other possibilities.

—Wilfred Sheed

The trouble with America is that there are far too many wide-open spaces surrounded by teeth.

—*Charles Luckman*

The thing that impresses me the most about America is the way parents obey their children.

—*King Edward VIII*

Sometimes I think this country would be better off if we could just saw off the eastern seaboard and let it float out to sea.

—*Barry Goldwater*

Speaking of New York, as a traveler I have two faults to find with it. In the first place there is nothing to see; and in the second place there is no mode of getting about to see anything.

—Anthony Trollope

If there was ever an aviary overstocked with jays it is that Yaptown on the Hudson called New York.

—O. Henry

New York is a different country. Maybe it ought to have a separate government. Everybody thinks differently, acts differently. They just don't know what the hell the rest of the United States is.

—Henry Ford

A car is useless in New York, essential everywhere else. The same with good manners.

—*Mignon McLaughlin*

A car is useless in New York, essential everywhere else. The same with good manners.

My only regret with Timothy McVeigh is he did not go to the New York Times Building.

—*Ann Coulter*

I love New York City; I've got a gun.

—*Charles Barkley*

New York is a city of seven million so decadent that when I leave it I never dare look back lest I turn into salt and the conductor throw me over his left shoulder for good luck.

—*Frank Sullivan*

Anytime four New Yorkers get into a cab together without arguing, a bank robbery has just taken place.

—*Johnny Carson*

New York now leads the world's great cities in the number of people around whom you shouldn't make a sudden move.

—*David Letterman*

I once spent a year in Philadelphia, I think it was on a Sunday.

—*W. C. Fields*

Washington, D.C. is a city of Southern efficiency and Northern charm.

—*John F. Kennedy*

How did it go in the madhouse? Rather badly. But in what other place could one live in America?

—*Ezra Pound, commenting upon his thirteen years in St. Elizabeth's Hospital in Washington, D.C.*

New Orleans is one of the two most ingrown, self-obsessed little cities in the United States. (The other is San Francisco.)

—*Nora Ephron*

San Francisco is a mad city—inhabited for the most part by perfectly insane people whose women are of a remarkable beauty.

—*Rudyard Kipling*

Fall is my favorite season in Los Angeles, watching the birds change color and fall from the trees.

—*David Letterman*

Hollywood is a sewer with service from the Ritz Carlton.

—*Wilson Mizner*

You can take all the sincerity in Hollywood, place it in the navel of a fruitfly and still have room for three caraway seeds and a producer's heart.

—Fred Allen

California is the only state in the union where you can fall asleep under a rose bush in full bloom and freeze to death.

—W. C. Fields

California is a fine place to live if you happen to be an orange.

—Fred Allen

If I owned Texas and Hell, I would rent out Texas and live in Hell.

—General Philip H. Sheridan

Here is the difference between Dante, Milton and me. They wrote about hell and never saw the place. I wrote about Chicago after looking the town over for years and years.

—*Carl Sandburg*

Miami Beach is where neon goes to die.

—*Lenny Bruce*

IV.

International Insults

Border Wars

Unmitigated noodles.

—*Kaiser Wilhelm II on England*

I know why the sun never sets on the British Empire: God wouldn't trust an Englishman in the dark.

—*Duncan Spaeth*

A demon took a monkey to wife—the results, by the grace of God, was the English.

—*Indian saying*

English coffee tastes like water that has been squeezed out of a wet sleeve.

—*Fred Allen*

The English think soap is civilization.

—*Heinrich von Treitschke*

The Englishman who has lost his fortune is said to have died of a broken heart.

—*Ralph Waldo Emerson*

Britain is the only country in the world where the food is more dangerous than the sex.

—*Jackie Mason*

Curse the blasted, jelly-boned swines, the slimy, the belly-wriggling invertebrates, the miserable soddingrotters, the flaming sods, the sniveling, dribbling, dithering, palsied, pulse-less lot that make up England today. They've got white of egg in their veins, and their spunk is that watery it's a marvel they can breed.

—*D. H. Lawrence*

When it's three o'clock in New York, it's still 1938 in London.

—*Bette Midler*

The way to endure summer in England is to have it framed and glazed in a comfortable room.

—*Horace Walpole*

The English country gentleman galloping after a fox—the unspeakable in full pursuit of the uneatable.

—*Oscar Wilde*

England, the heart of a rabbit in the body of a lion. The jaws of a serpent, in an abode of popinjays.

—*Eugene Deschamps*

If one could teach the English to talk and the Irish to listen, society would be quite civilised.

—*Oscar Wilde*

Give an Irishman lager for a month, and he's a dead man. An Irishman is lined with copper, and the beer corrodes it, but whiskey polishes the copper and is the saving of him.

—*Mark Twain*

Put an Irishman on a spit and you can always find another one to turn him.

—*George Bernard Shaw*

Other people have a nationality. The Irish and the Jews have a psychosis.

—*Brendan Behan*

As sluttish and slatternly as an Irishwoman bred in France.

—*Irish saying*

Ireland is the sow that eats her farrow.

—*James Joyce*

The Irish are a fair people, they never speak well of one another.

—*Samuel Johnson*

Like an Irishman's obligation, all on the one side, and always yours.

—*English saying*

For the Irish, there are no stars in the sky.

—*English saying*

This is one race of people for whom psychoanalysis is of no use whatsoever.

—*Sigmund Freud (about the Irish)*

The trouble with Ireland is that it's a country full of genius, with absolutely no talent.

—*Hugh Leonard*

The noblest prospect which a Scotchman ever sees, is the high road that leads him to England.

—*Samuel Johnson*

Scotland: A land of meanness, sophistry and lust.

—Lord Byron

Scotland: That garret of the earth—that knuckle-end of England—that land of Calvin, oatcakes, and sulfur.

—Sydney Smith

Asked by a Scot what Johnson thought of Scotland: "That it is a very vile country, to be sure, Sir."

"Well, Sir! (replies the Scot, somewhat mortified), God made it."

Johnson: "Certainly he did; but we must always remember that he made it for Scotchmen, and comparisons are odious, Mr. S———; but God made hell."

—James Boswell, in his Life of Samuel Johnson

The great thing about Glasgow now is that if there is a nuclear attack it'll look exactly the same afterwards.

—*Billy Connolly*

He who would eat in Spain must bring his kitchen along.

—*German saying*

A Spaniard may be trusted, but no further than your nose.

—*German saying*

Spaniards are like lice: once they are there, it is difficult to get rid of them.

—*German saying*

A Spaniard and a braggart are the same thing.

—*German saying*

If the French were really intelligent, they'd speak English.

—*Wilfred Sheed*

France is a dog hole, and it no more merits the tread of a man's foot.

—*William Shakespeare*

It took no more effort than casting a Frenchman into Hell.

—*Dutch saying*

France is a country where the money falls apart in your hands and you can't tear the toilet paper.

—*Billy Wilder*

The French are sawed-off sissies who eat snails and slugs and cheese that smells like people's feet. Utter cowards who force their own children to drink wine, they gibber like baboons even when you try to speak to them in their own wimpy language.

—*P. J. O'Rourke*

The friendship of the French is like their wine, exquisite, but of short duration.

—*German saying*

Paris is like a whore, from a distance she seems ravishing, you can't wait until you have her in your arms. Five minutes later you feel empty, disgusted with yourself. You feel tricked.

—*Henry Miller*

A fighting Frenchman runs away from even a she-goat.

—*Russian saying*

I do not dislike the French from the vulgar antipathy between neighboring nations, but for their insolent and unfounded airs of superiority.

—*Horace Walpole*

The German may be a good fellow, but it is best to hang him just the same.

—*Russian saying*

Germany, the diseased world's bathhouse.

—*Mark Twain*

One thing I will say about the Germans, they are always perfectly willing to give somebody's land to somebody else.

—*Will Rogers*

Marry a German and you'll see that the woman have hairy tongues.

—*Rumanian saying*

I speak Spanish to God, Italian to women, French to men, and German to my horse.

—*Emperor Charles V*

German is a language which was developed solely to afford the speaker the opportunity to spit at strangers under the guise of polite conversation.

—National Lampoon

Because of their cuisine, Germans don't consider farting rude. They'd certainly be out of luck if they did.

—*P. J. O'Rourke*

German is the most extravagantly ugly language—it sounds like someone using a sick bag on a 747.

—*Willy Rushton*

The German mind has a talent for making no mistakes but the very greatest.

—*Clifton Fadiman*

You can always reason with a German. You can always reason with a barnyard animal, too, for all the good it does.

—*P.J. O'Rourke*

The Germans are like women. You can scarcely ever fathom their depths—they haven't any.

—Friedrich Wilhelm Nietzsche

If there is a Hell, Rome is built on top of it.

—German saying

Rome reminds me of a man who lives by exhibiting to travelers his grandmother's corpse.

—James Joyce

Half an Italian in a house is one too many.

—German saying

There are two Italies. . . . The one is the most sublime and lovely contemplation that can be conceived by the imagination of man; the other is the most degraded, disgusting, and odious. What do you think? Young women of rank actually eat—you will never guess what—garlick! Our poor friend Lord Byron is quite corrupted by living among these people, and in fact, is going on in a way not worthy of him.

—Percy Bysshe Shelley

Italian soup.

—Czech term for poison

Q. How many Italians does it take to screw in a light bulb?

A. Two. One to screw it in, and the other to shoot the witness.

Cross yourself once before an Andalusian and thrice on spotting an Italian.

—*Spanish saying*

The Japanese have perfected good manners and made them indistinguishable from rudeness.

—*Paul Theroux*

There are only two kinds of Chinese—those who give bribes, and those who take them.

—*Russian saying*

I found the pearl of the Orient slightly less exciting than a rainy Sunday evening in Rochester.

—S. J. Perelman

Harbin is now being called the Chicago of the East. This is not a compliment to Chicago.

—Maurice Baring

How can you tell a Russian? Go to sleep and he will rob you.

—Ukrainian saying

In Russia a man is called reactionary if he objects to having his property stolen and his wife and children murdered.

—*Winston Churchill*

Russians will consume marinated mushrooms and vodka, salted herring and vodka, smoked salmon and vodka, salami and vodka, caviar on brown bread and vodka, pickled cucumbers and vodka, cold tongue and vodka, red beet salad and vodka, scallions and vodka—anything and everything and vodka.

—*Hedrick Smith*

If a Russian is in the hills, count your olives.

—*Greek saying*

Better the devil in your house than a Russian.

—*Ukrainian saying*

Holland is a country where the earth is better than the air; where profit is sought more than honor; where there is more sense than esprit, more goodwill than good humor, more prosperity than pleasure and where a visit is preferable to a stay for life.

—*German saying*

The indigested vomit of the sea/ Fell to the Dutch by just propriety.

—*Andrew Marvell*

God made serpents and rabbits and Armenians.

—*Turkish saying*

The food in Yugoslavia is fine if you like pork tartare.

—*Ed Begley, Jr.*

Few things can be less tempting or dangerous than a Greek woman of the age of thirty.

—*John Carne*

Canada could have had French culture, American know-how, and English government. Instead it got French government, English know-how, and American culture.

—*John Colombo*

Canada is a country so square that even the female impersonators are women.

—*Richard Brenner*

I fear that I have not got much to say about Canada, not having seen much; what I got by going to Canada was a cold.

—*Henry David Thoreau*

Germans are flummoxed by humor, the Swiss have no concept of fun, the Spanish think there is nothing at all ridiculous about eating dinner at midnight, and the Italians should never, ever have been let in on the invention of the motor car.

—*Bill Bryson*

In America, only the successful writer is important, in France all writers are important, in England no writer is important, and in Australia you have to explain what a writer is.

—*Geoffrey Cottrell*

There have been many definitions of hell, but for the English the best definition is that it is the place where the Germans are the police, the Swedish are the comedians, the Italians are the defense force, Frenchmen dig the roads, the Belgians are the pop singers, the Spanish run the railways, the Turks cook the food, the Irish are the waiters, the Greeks run the government, and the common language is Dutch.

—*Sir David Frost*

And while we're examining other cultures, how about a few insults and curses:

YIDDISH

He should grow upside down with his head in the ground like a turnip.

All problems I have in my heart, should go to his head.

Let what I wish on him come true—most, even half, even just 10 per cent.

One misfortune is too few for him.

He should marry the daughter of the Angel of Death.

He should give it all away to doctors.

Let him suffer and remember.

He should laugh with lizards.

They should free a madman, and lock him up.

I should outlive him long enough to bury him.

He should have a large store, and whatever people ask for he shouldn't have, and what he does have shouldn't be requested.

He should be transformed into a chandelier, to hang by day and to burn by night.

He should have Pharaoh's plagues sprinkled with Job's scabies.

He should have a lawsuit in which he knows he is right.

May he have a million dollars, and may it not be enough to pay his doctor bills.

Irish

May the curse of Mary Malone and her nine blind illegitimate children chase you so far over the hills of Damnation that the Lord himself can't find you with a telescope.

May you melt off the earth like snow off the ditch.

Gypsy

May you wander over the face of the earth forever, never sleep twice in the same bed, never drink water twice from the same well, and never cross the same river twice in a year.

CHINESE

I wish you a slow death, but a quick ride to hell!

May you live in interesting times.

V.

Sports

Brickbats and Balls

Fly fishing may be a very pleasant amusement; but angling or float fishing I can only compare to a stick and a string, with a worm at one end and a fool at the other.

—*Samuel Johnson*

Fishing is boring, unless you catch an actual fish, and then it is disgusting.

—*Dave Barry*

I went to a fight the other night, and a hockey game broke out.

—*Rodney Dangerfield*

All hockey players are bilingual. They know English and profanity.

—*Gordie Howe*

Hockey is a sport for white men. Basketball is a sport for black men. Golf is a sport for white men dressed like black pimps.

—*Tiger Woods*

Although golf was originally restricted to wealthy, overweight Protestants, today it's open to anybody who owns hideous clothing.

—*Dave Barry*

The only time he opens his mouth is to change feet.

—*David Feherty on fellow golfer Nick Faldo*

He has a face like a warthog that's been stung by a wasp.

—*David Feherty on fellow golfer Colin Montgomerie*

She's about as cuddly as a dead hedgehog. The Alsatians in her yard would go about in pairs for protection.

—*jockey John Francombe on racehorse trainer Jenny Pitman*

Cross country skiing is great if you live in a small country.

—*Steven Wright*

Dennis has become like a prostitute, but now it's gotten ridiculous, to the point where he will do anything humanly possible to make money.

—*Charles Barkley on basketball player Dennis Rodman*

Basketball, a game which won't be fit for people until they set the basket umbilicus-high and return the giraffes to the zoo.

—*Ogden Nash*

He couldn't bowl a hoop downhill.

—*Fred Trueman on cricketer Ian Botham*

A lot of people are using two-piece cues nowadays. Alex Higgins hasn't got one because they don't come with instructions.

—*Steve Davis on snooker world champion, Alex Higgins*

Like a Volvo, Björn Borg is rugged, has good after sales service, and is very dull.

—*Clive James on tennis star Björn Borg*

Martina [Navratilova] was so far in the closet she was in danger of being a garment bag.

—*Rita Mae Brown*

McEnroe was as charming as always, which means that he was as charming as a dead mouse in a loaf of bread.

—*Clive James on tennis star (and temperamental) John McEnroe*

I'm not having points taken off me by an incompetent old fool. You're the pits of the world.

—*John McEnroe to an umpire*

You can't see as well as these fucking flowers—and they're fucking plastic.

—*John McEnroe to a line judge*

What other problems do you have besides being unemployed, a moron and a dork?

—*John McEnroe to a spectator*

According to the *Express*, Kevin Keegan will star in an advertising campaign aimed at tempting people back to church this Christmas. Presumably Keggy was hired because of the way his Euro 2000 team inspired twenty million watching Englishmen to shout "Jesus Christ!" in unison.

—*Mediawatch on Football365.com*

Kevin Keegan isn't fit to lace my boots—or my whiskies.

—*Soccer star George Best*

Lord Nelson! Lord Beaverbrook! Sir Winston Churchill! Sir Anthony Eden! Clement Attlee! Henry Cooper! Lady Diana! Maggie Thatcher—can you hear me, Maggie Thatcher! . . . Your boys took one hell of a beating!

—*Norwegian sports commentator Bjørge Lillelien after Norway beat England in a soccer match*

Footballers are only interested in drinking, clothes, and the size of their willies.

—*Karen Brady, managing director of Birmingham City soccer club (and married to a soccer player)*

I don't think heading the ball has got anything to do with it. Footballers are stupid enough anyway.

—*British Premier League spokesman responding to a report that brain cells are damaged by heading the ball*

Somebody compared him to Billy McNeil, but I don't remember Billy being crap.

—*Tommy Docherty on British soccer player Lorenzo Amoruso*

The bad news for Saddam Hussein is that he's just been sentenced to the death penalty. The good news for Saddam is that David Beckham is taking it.

—*anonymous British soccer commentator*

Football combines the two worst features of American life: it is violence punctuated by committee meetings.

—*George Will*

If a man watches three football games in a row, he should be declared legally dead.

—*Erma Bombeck*

Football is a game designed to keep coal miners off the streets.

—*Jimmy Breslin*

[Boxer] Trevor Brooking floats like a butterfly and stings like one too.

—*Brian Clough*

He is phony, using his blackness to get his way.

—*Joe Frazier on Muhammad Ali*

Joe Frazier is so ugly he should donate his face to the U.S. Bureau of Wildlife.

—*Muhammad Ali*

[He's] so ugly, when he sweats the sweat runs backwards over his head to avoid his face!

—Muhammad Ali on an opponent

Sometimes Howard makes me wish I was a dog, and he was a fireplug.

—Muhammad Ali on sports commentator Howard Cosell

You! You're the child who rhapsodizes about the infield-fly rule. I'm sure you'll have a fine career.

—Howard Cosell to sportscaster Bob Costas

I did not call [Boston Red Sox manager Darrell] Johnson an idiot. Someone else did, and I just agreed.

—*pitcher Jim Palmer at the All-Star Game*

George Steinbrenner is the center of evil in the universe.

—*Ben Affleck on the New York Yankees owner*

One's a born liar, and the other's been convicted.

—*Billy Martin on New York Yankee superstar Reggie Jackson and owner George Steinbrenner*

With the A's, we depended upon pitching and speed to win. With the Giants, we depended upon pitching and power to win. With the Indians, we depended upon an act of God.

—*baseball manager Alvin Dark, reviewing his career*

If I could hit the ball that way, I'd take off my toeplate and retire from pitching. In fact, if I hit the way you do, I think I'd also retire from baseball.

—*baseball pitcher Bob Gibson to teammate Curt Flood during batting practice*

Major league baseball has asked its players to stop tossing baseballs into the stands during games, because they say fans fight over them and they get hurt. In fact, the Florida Marlins said that's why they never hit any home runs. It's a safety issue.

—*Jay Leno*

I don't know but somebody told me they were waiters at the Last Supper.

—*Los Angeles Dodgers manager Tommy Lasorda when asked the ages of two veteran pitchers*

Hey Boston, Now You Know What It Feels Like To Be A Yankee

—*Tee-shirt message after the Boston Red Sox won the 2004 World Series*

Q: What do the Red Sox and lawn furniture have in common?

A: They both fold and end up in the cellar after Labor Day.

—*applicable before 2004*

The Chicago Cubs, which hasn't won a World Series since 1908 and last appeared in a Series in 1945, have produced a plethora of jibes. Here are some of the choice ones:

It's hard to put your finger on it. You have to have a dullness of mind and spirit to play here. I went through psychoanalysis and that helped me deal with my Cubness.

—Jim Brosnan, former Cubs pitcher

Noise pollution can't be that much of a problem. There's nothing to cheer about.

—State Representative John F. Dunn arguing for the installation of lights at Wrigley Field

If I managed the Cubs, I'd be an alcoholic.

—Whitey Herzog

There's nothing wrong with this team that more pitching, more fielding, and more hitting couldn't help.

—Bill Buckner

You get tired of looking at garbage in your own backyard.

—manager Lee Elia, explaining why the Cubs traded so many players in 1983 (Elia was fired later that year)

The Cubs were taking batting practice, and the pitching machine threw a no-hitter.

—anonymous radio announcer

Would the lady who left her nine kids at Wrigley Field please pick them up immediately? They are beating the Cubs 4–0 in the seventh inning.

—radio deejay

One thing you learn as a Cubs fan: When you bought your ticket, you could bank on seeing the bottom of the ninth.

—announcer Joe Garagiola

Q: Did you hear about the new Cubs soup?

A: Two sips and then you choke.

The latest diet is better than the Pritikin Diet: You eat only when the Cubs win.

—pianist George Shearing

Heckles to Sports Teams

This team couldn't beat anything with a stick.

Maybe this team are all left-handed and they don't know it.

I hope this team paid to get in.

You guys would be out of your depth in a parking lot puddle.

Do this team actually practice or do they just show up for the games?

This team couldn't make ice without a recipe.

Hurry up and practice, the game has started.

I've got a better team pulling my sleigh.

Do you think this team will like this game once they catch on?

Did this team sign a contract with Palmolive Soap? They're all washed up.

This team should go back to the minors.

Does this team think it's "Ladies Night" out there?

Is this team going to play the whole game today?

Bring out the elephants; the clowns are already here.

Do you want *my* autograph?

Heckles to Umpires and Referees

Hey, Mr. Magoo, did you forget your glasses?

You couldn't make the right call if you had a phone book.

I've seen potatoes with better eyes.

If you had one more eye you'd be a Cyclops.

I thought only horses slept standing up!

If I had a dollar for every good call you've made, I'd be broke!

Now I know why there's only one "I" in umpire

If you're just going to watch the game, buy a ticket.

They're putting your strike zone on the back of milk cartons.

I was confused the first time I saw a game too.

I've gotten better calls from my ex-wife!

Does your wife let you make decisions at home?

VI.

MUSIC

Rhythm and Boos

Elvis transcends his talent to the point of dispensing with it altogether.

—Greil Marcus about Elvis Presley

Presley sounded like Jayne Mansfield looked—blowsy and loud and low.

—Julie Burchill

He plays four-and-a-half-hour sets. That's torture. Does he hate his audience?

—John Lydon about Bruce Springsteen

He has Van Gogh's ear for music.

—Orson Welles on '70s pop star Donny Osmond

She ought to be arrested for loitering in front of an orchestra.

—*Bette Midler on Helen Reddy*

It's too late to apologize.

—*Arturo Toscanini, retort to the insult "Nuts to you!" shouted at him by a player he had just ordered from the stage during rehearsal*

. . . glorified bandmaster.

—*Sir Thomas Beecham on Arturo Toscanini*

One had the feeling that underneath there was something false. His speech was particularly affected. . . . He gave the impression of a glittering, multi-coloured painted shell; when one looked inside one found an infinite emptiness.

—Massimo Freccia on conductor Leopold Stokowski

Beethoven's last quartets were written by a deaf man and should only be listened to by a deaf man.

—Sir Thomas Beecham on Ludwig van Beethoven

Beethoven always sounds like the upsetting of bags—with here and there a dropped hammer.

—John Ruskin

By God, no—if it had been, I should have run away myself.

—The Duke of Wellington, when asked whether Beethoven's Battle Symphony was like the actual battle of Waterloo

I liked your opera. I think I'll set it to music.

—Ludwig van Beethoven to a fellow composer

Berlioz composes by splashing his pen over the manuscript and leaving the issue to chance.

—Frederic Chopin on Hector Berlioz

I can compare *Le Carnival Romain* by Berlioz to nothing but the caperings and gibberings of a big baboon, over-excited by a dose of alcoholic stimulus.

—George Templeton Strong

A tub of pork and beer.

—Hector Berlioz on George Frederick Handel

If he'd been making shell cases during the war it might have been better for music.

—Camille Saint-Saens on Maurice Ravel

The difference between a violin and a viola is that a viola burns longer.

—*Victor Borge*

If I don't practice for one day, I know it; two days, the public knows it; three days, the critics know it.

—*Jascha Heifetz*

Difficult do you call it, Sir? I wish it were impossible.

—*Samuel Johnson, on hearing a famous violinist*

Jack Benny played Mendelssohn last night. Mendelssohn lost.

—*Anonymous*

It gives us, for the first time, the hideous notion that there can be music which stinks to the ear.

—Eduardo Hanslick on Pyotr Illyich Tchaikovsky's Violin Concerto

What a giftless bastard!

—Pyotr Illyich Tchaikovsky on Johannes Brahms

Handel is only fourth rate. He is not even interesting.

— Pyotr Illyich Tchaikovsky on George Frederick Handel

One feels that the composer must have made a bet, for all his professional reputation was worth, that he would write the most hideous thing that had ever been put on paper, and he won it, too.

—Boston Evening Transcript
reviewing Tchaikovsky's Slavonic March

I wish the government would put a tax on pianos for the incompetent.

—*Dame Edith Sitwell*

I suffered more than upon any occasion in my life apart from an incident or two connected with "painless dentistry."

—*Percy Scholes on a Bartok piano concerto*

A composer for one right hand.

—Richard Wagner on Frederic Chopin

Is Wagner actually a man? Is he not rather a disease? Everything he touches falls ill: he has made music sick.

—Friedrich Wilhelm Nietzsche on Richard Wagner

I have witnessed and greatly enjoyed the first act of everything which Wagner created, but the effect on me has always been so powerful that one act was quite sufficient; whenever I have witnessed two acts I have gone away physically exhausted; and whenever I have ventured an entire opera the result has been the next thing to suicide.

—Mark Twain

I love Wagner, but the music I prefer is that of a cat hung up by its tail outside a window and trying to stick to the panes of glass with its claws.

—*Charles Baudelaire on Richard Wagner*

Wagner has lovely moments but awful quarters of an hour.

—*Gioacchino Rossini*

Of all the bete, clumsy, blundering, boggling, baboon-blooded stuff that I ever saw on a human stage, that last night beat—as far as the story and acting went—all the affected, sapless, soulless, beginningless, endless, topless, bottomless, topsiturviest, tuneless, scrabble-pipiest-tongs and boniest-doggerel of sounds I ever endured the deadliness of, that eternity of nothing was deadliest, as far as its sound went.

—*John Ruskin on Richard Wagner*

Wagner's music is better than it sounds.

—*Mark Twain*

The tone-picture, with all its abnormal and hideously grotesque proportions, is that of a heavy, dull and witless Teuton. The orchestration of the work is sound and fury, signifying nothing, and the instruments are made to indulge in a shrieking, piercing, noisy breakdown most of the time.

—*review of the American premiere of* Till Eulenspiegel *by Richard Strauss*

I don't mind what language an opera is sung in so long as it is a language I don't understand.

—*Sir Edward Appleton*

No opera plot can be sensible, for people do not sing when they are feeling sensible.

—*W. H. Auden*

Anything too stupid to be said is sung.

—*Voltaire*

Roseanne Barr's singing the national anthem was my cat being neutered.

—*Johnny Carson*

He sang like a hinge.

—*Ethel Merman on Cole Porter*

Her voice sounded like an eagle being goosed.

—*Ralph Novak on Yoko Ono*

Actually, I never liked Dylan's kind of music before; I always thought he sounded just like Yogi Bear.

—*Mick Ronson*

The sheets of sound they let loose have the cumulative effect of mugging.

—The London Times *on the Clash*

Where did these turkeys learn to write music, anyway?

—*review in* Comoedia *of Igor Stravinsky's* The Rite of Spring

I had no idea Stravinsky disliked Debussy as much as this.

—Musical Times *review of Igor Stravinsky's "Symphony for Wind: In Memory of Debussy"*

His music used to be original. Now it's aboriginal.

—Sir Ernest Newman on Igor Stravinsky

I don't want to make a cemetery of your composition.

—Johannes Brahms, to composer Hugo Wolf, who had sent Brahms the sheet music to a song with the request that Brahms mark a cross wherever he found a fault

Listening to the Fifth Symphony of Ralph Vaughan Williams is like staring at a cow for forty-five minutes.

—*Aaron Copland*

All Bach's last movements are like the running of a sewing machine.

—*Arnold Bax on Johann Sebastian Bach*

Someone asked Milton Berle, "What kind of cigar are you smoking there?"

"It's a Lawrence Welk."

"What's a Lawrence Welk?"

"It's a piece of crap with a band wrapped around it."

If he ever gets out of the key of E, he might be dangerous.

—Jerry Lee Lewis on Bo Diddley

Jazz: Music invented for the torture of imbeciles.

—Henry Van Dyke

I don't like country music—but don't mean to denigrate those who do. For those who like country music, denigrate means "to put down."

—Bob Newhart

When you talk to him, he looks at you and grins and grins and nods and nods and appears to be the world's best listener, until you realize he is not listening at all.

—Larry L. King on Willie Nelson

Q: How can you tell the difference between bluegrass songs?

A: By their titles.

I could eat alphabet soup and shit better lyrics.

—*composer Johnny Mercer, commenting on a British musical*

It is quite untrue that British people don't appreciate music. They may not understand it but they absolutely love the noise it makes.

—*Sir Thomas Beecham*

She's got a face like a satellite dish and ankles like my granny's.

—*Robbie Williams on British pop star Sophie Ellis Bextor*

He has become the oldest living cute boy in the world.

—*Anna Quindlen about Paul McCartney*

He could be a maneuvering swine, which no one ever realized.

—*Paul McCartney on John Lennon*

Bad-mannered little shits.

—*Noel Coward on the Beatles*

We idolized the Beatles, except for those of us who idolized the Rolling Stones, who in those days still had many of their original teeth.

—*Dave Barry*

I think Mick Jagger would be astounded and amazed if he realized to how many people he is not a sex symbol but a mother image.

—*David Bowie*

He moves like a parody between a majorette girl and Fred Astaire.

—*Truman Capote on Mick Jagger*

He's about as sexy as a pissing toad.

—*Truman Capote on Mick Jagger*

I'm glad I've given up drugs and alcohol. It would be awful to be like Keith Richards. He's pathetic. It's like a monkey with arthritis, trying to go on stage and look young. I have great respect for the Stones but they would have been better if they had thrown Keith out fifteen years ago.

—*Elton John about Keith Richards*

His writing is limited to songs for dead blondes.

—*Keith Richards about Elton John*

I love [his] work but I couldn't warm to him even if I was cremated next to him.

—Keith Richards on Chuck Berry

He's a wimp in disguise. He should go home and shave.

—Keith Richards on George Michael

Sleeping with George Michael would be like having sex with a groundhog.

—Boy George

Boy George is all England needs—another queen who can't dress.

—Joan Rivers

He looks like a dwarf who's been dipped in a bucket of pubic hair.

—Boy George on Prince

Bambi with testosterone.

—Owen Gleiberman about Prince

Michael Jackson's album was only called "Bad" because there wasn't enough room on the sleeve for "Pathetic."

—Prince

He now looks like a Barbie doll that has been whittled at by a malicious brother.

—Thomas Sutcliffe about Michael Jackson

He sings like he's throwing up.

—*Andrew O'Connor about Bryan Ferry*

He sounds like he's got a brick dangling from his willy, and a food-mixer making purée of his tonsils.

—*Paul Lester about Jon Bon Jovi*

He was so mean it hurt him to go to the bathroom.

—*Britt Eklund about Rod Stewart*

They want to play the blues so badly, and that's how they play it—badly!
—*bluesman Sonny Boy Williams on the rock group the Yardbirds*

Is he just doing a bad Elvis pout, or was he born that way?
—*Freddie Mercury on Billy Idol*

I love it when someone insults me. That means that I don't have to be nice anymore.
—*Billy Idol*

And some slams at instruments and the people who play them:

Why do some people take an instant aversion to banjo players?

It saves time.

Banjo players spend half their lives tuning and the other half playing out of tune.

How is lightning like a violist's fingers?

Neither one strikes in the same place twice.

Did you hear about the bassist who was so out of tune the bass section noticed?

What's the definition of a quarter tone?

A harpist tuning unison strings.

What is the definition of a half step?

Two oboes playing in unison.

What's the difference between a baritone saxophone and a chain saw?

The exhaust.

Definition of a gentleman: someone who can play the bagpipes but doesn't.

What's the difference between trumpet players and government bonds?

Government bonds eventually mature and earn money.

How do you know when a trombone player is at your door?

The doorbell drags.

Why is the French horn a divine instrument?

Because a man blows in it, but only God knows what comes out of it.

Why are orchestra intermissions limited to twenty minutes?

So you don't have to retrain the drummers.

How do you get a guitar player to play softer?

Give him some sheet music.

VII.

Politics *and* History

Outrage Through the Ages

You have all the characteristics of a popular politician: a horrible voice, bad breeding, and a vulgar manner.

—*Aristophanes*

He knows nothing and thinks he knows everything. That points clearly to a political career.

—*George Bernard Shaw*

Reader, suppose you were an idiot; and suppose you were a member of Congress; but I repeat myself.

—*Mark Twain*

They never open their mouths without subtracting from the sum of human knowledge.

—*Speaker of the House Thomas Reed of two fellow congressmen*

Here richly, with ridiculous display,
The Politician's corpse was laid away.
While all of his acquaintance sneered and slanged
I wept: for I had longed to see him hanged.

—*Hilaire Belloc, "Epitaph on the Politician"*

He is racist, he's homophobic, he's xenophobic and he's a sexist. He's the perfect Republican candidate.

—*Bill Press about Pat Buchanan*

The Democrats are the party that says government will make you smarter, taller, richer, and remove the crabgrass on your lawn. The Republicans are the party that says government doesn't work and then they get elected and prove it.

—*P. J. O'Rourke*

The Democrats seem to be basically nicer people, but they have demonstrated time and again that they have the management skills of celery.

—*Dave Barry*

Any political party that can't cough up anything better than a treacherous brain-damaged old vulture like Hubert Humphrey deserves every beating it gets. They don't hardly make 'em like Hubert any more—but just to be on the safe side, he should be castrated anyway.

—*Hunter S. Thompson on Vice President Hubert Humphrey*

An empty suit that goes to funerals and plays golf.

—Ross Perot on Vice President Dan Quayle

When Al Gore gives a fireside chat, the fire goes out.

—Bob Dole

He can compress the most words into the smallest idea of any man I know.

—Abraham Lincoln on a political opponent

His argument is as thin as the . . . soup that was made by boiling the shadow of a pigeon that had been starved to death.

—Abraham Lincoln on Stephen A. Douglas

I never thought him an honest, frank-dealing man, but considered him as a crooked gun, . . . whose aim or shot you could never be sure of.

—Thomas Jefferson on Aaron Burr

A rigid, fanatic, ambitious, selfishly partisan and sectional turncoat with too much genius and too little common sense, who will either die a traitor or a madman.

—Henry Clay on John C. Calhoun

He is, like almost all the eminent men of this country, only half educated. His morals, public and private, are loose.

—John Quincy Adams on Henry Clay

. . . the most meanly and foolishly treacherous man I ever heard of.

—*James Russell Lowell on Daniel Webster*

The word *liberty* in the mouth of Mr. Webster sounds like the word *love* in the mouth of a courtesan.

—*Ralph Waldo Emerson*

God made the Idiot for practice, and then He made the School Board.

—*Mark Twain*

He has all the characteristics of a dog except loyalty.

—*Sam Houston on Thomas Jefferson Green*

He's the only man able to walk under a bed without hitting his head.

—*Walter Winchell on presidential candidate Thomas E. Dewey*

You really have to get to know him to dislike him.

—*James T. Patterson on Thomas E. Dewey*

He is just about the nastiest little man I've ever known. He struts sitting down.

—Lillian Dykstra on Thomas E. Dewey

The Wizard of Ooze.

—John F. Kennedy on Speaker of the House Everett Dirksen

The hustler from Chicago.

—George H. W. Bush on the Reverend Jesse Jackson

His mind was like a soup dish, wide and shallow; it could hold a small amount of nearly anything, but the slightest jarring spilled the soup into somebody's lap.

—novelist Irving Stone on William Jennings Bryan

He no play-a the game, he no make-a the rules.

—Secretary of Agriculture Earl Butz on Pope Pius XII's attitude toward birth control

He's thin boys. He's thin as piss on a hot rock.

—Senator William F. Jenner on governor and diplomat W. Averell Harriman

Marion Barry at the Million Man March—you know what that means? That means even at our finest hour, we had a crackhead on stage.

—*Chris Rock on Washington, D.C., mayor Marion Barry, who went to prison on a cocaine-possession conviction*

Magic Johnson, former basketball player, may run for mayor of LA in the next election. Remember the good 'ol days when only qualified people ran for office like actors and professional wrestlers?

—*Jay Leno*

What makes him think a middle-aged actor, who's played with a chimp, could have a future in politics?

—*Ronald Reagan on Clint Eastwood's Carmel, California, mayoral bid*

He is suffering from halitosis of the intellect. That's presuming he has intellect.

—*Harold Ickes on Louisiana governor Huey Long*

It was hard to listen to Goldwater and realize that a man could be half Jewish and yet sometimes appear twice as dense as the normal Gentile.

—*I. F. Stone on Senator Barry Goldwater*

Don't be so humble, you're not that great.

—*Golda Meir to Moshe Dayan*

. . . a blooded, calculating unprincipled Usurper, without a virtue, no statesman, knowing nothing of commerce, political economy, or civil government, and supplying ignorance by bold presumption.

—*Thomas Jefferson on Napoleon Bonaparte*

Strip your Louis Quatorze of his king gear, and there is left nothing but a poor forked radish with a head fantastically carved.

—*Thomas Carlyle on King Louis XIV of France*

The Right Honourable Gentleman is indebted to his memory for his jests and to his imagination for his facts.

—*Richard Brinsley Sheridan on the Earl of Dundas*

A pig, an ass, a dunghill, the spawn of an adder, a basilisk, a lying buffoon, a mad fool with a frothy mouth.

—Martin Luther on King Henry VIII

. . The plain truth is, that he was a most intolerable ruffian, a disgrace to human nature, and a blot of blood and grease upon the history of England.

—Charles Dickens on King Henry VIII

You have sent me a Flanders mare.

—King Henry VIII to a courtier, on seeing his fourth wife, Anne of Cleves, for the first time

As just and merciful as Nero and as good a Christian as Mohammed.

—*John Wesley on Queen Elizabeth I*

I cannot find it in me to fear a man who took ten years a-learning of his alphabet.

—*Queen Elizabeth I on King Philip II of Spain*

The wisest fool in Christendom.

—*King Henri IV of France on King James I of England*

Here lies our mutton-loving king, Whose word no man relies on;
Who never said a foolish thing, And never did a wise one.

—*John Wilmot, Earl of Rochester on King Charles II*

She was happy as the dey was long.

—*Lord Norbury on Queen Caroline's affair with the Dey of Algiers*

My dear firstborn is the greatest ass, and the greatest liar and the greatest canaille and the greatest beast in the whole world and I most heartily wish he were out of it.

—*Queen Caroline on her son Frederick, Prince of Wales*

Here lies Fred, Who was alive and now is dead: Had it been his father, I had much rather; Had it been his brother, Better than another; Had it been his sister, No one would have missed her; Had it been the whole generation, Better for the nation: But since 'tis only Fred, Who was alive and is dead—There's no more to be said.

—*Horace Walpole on Frederick, Prince of Wales*

. . . An Adonis of fifty . . . a violator of his word, a libertine over head and ears in debt and disgrace, a despiser of domestic ties, the companion of gamblers and demi-reps, a man without a single claim to the gratitude of his country or the respect of posterity . . .

—*Leigh Hunt on the Prince of Wales, later George IV*

A more contemptible, cowardly, selfish unfeeling dog does not exist than this king . . . with vices and weaknesses of the lowest and most contemptible order.

—*Charles Greville on King George IV*

Alvanley—who's your fat friend?

—*George Beau Brummel on George IV*

George the First was always reckoned Vile, but viler George the Second; And what mortal ever heard any good from George the Third? When from Earth the Fourth descended (God be praised!) the Georges ended.

—*Walter Savage Landor on the first four English King Georges*

Nowadays a parlor maid as ignorant as Queen Victoria was when she came to the throne would be classed as mentally defective.

—*George Bernard Shaw on Queen Victoria*

Born into the ranks of the working class, the new King's most likely fate would have been that of a street-corner loafer.

—James Keir Hardie on King George V

His intellect is of no more use than a pistol packed in the bottom of a trunk in the robber infested Apennines.

—Prince Albert on his son Edward, Prince of Wales, later King Edward VII

A pimple on the arse of the Empire.

—Count Alfred de Marigny, referring to the Duke of Windsor, formerly King Edward VIII

In defeat he was unbeatable; in victory, unbearable.

—Edward Marsh on Field Marshal the Viscount Montgomery of Alamein

Never trust a man who combs his hair straight from his left armpit.

—Alice Roosevelt Longworth on General Douglas MacArthur

MacArthur is the type of man who thinks that when he gets to heaven, God will step down from the great white throne and bow him into his vacated seat.

—Harold Ickes on General Douglas MacArthur

The General is suffering from mental saddle sores.

—Harold L. Ickes on Hugh S. Johnson

Dangerous as an enemy, untrustworthy as a friend, but fatal as a colleague.

—Sir Hercules Robinson on British statesman Joseph Chamberlain

Canada has at last produced a political leader worthy of assassination.

—Irving Layton on Canadian Prime Minister Pierre Trudeau

It is better to be sincere in one language than to be a twit in two.

—*Transport Minister John Crosbie about Pierre Trudeau*

The Honourable Member disagrees. I can hear him shaking his head.

—*Pierre Trudeau, replying to a question in Parliament*

Little chubby little sucker.

—*Reform MP Darrell Stinson about Progressive Conservative Leader Jean Charest*

Frankly, if I was going to recruit somebody, I'd go further up the gene pool.

—Liberal cabinet minister Reg Alcock when asked whether he offered an ambassadorship to Tory MP Inky Mark

He has sat on the fence so long that the iron has entered his soul.

—British Prime Minister David Lloyd George

He is brilliant—to the top of his boots.

—David Lloyd George

Oh, if I could piss the way he speaks!

—Georges Clemenceau on David Lloyd George

One could not even dignify him with the name of stuffed shirt. He was simply a hole on the air.

—George Orwell on British Prime Minister Stanley Baldwin

We know that he has, more than any other man, the gift of compressing the largest amount of words into the smallest amount of thought.

—Sir Winston Churchill on British Prime Minister Ramsay MacDonald

He has the lucidity which is the byproduct of a fundamentally sterile mind.

—Aneurin Bevan on British Prime Minister Neville Chamberlain

He has devoted the best years of his life to preparing his impromptu speeches.

—*Earl of Birkenhead on Sir Winston Churchill*

He would kill his own mother just so that he could use her skin to make a drum to beat his own praises.

—*Margot Asquith on Sir Winston Churchill*

He has all the virtues I dislike and none of the vices I admire.

—*attributed to Sir Winston Churchill*

Attila the Hen.

—Clement Freud on British Prime Minister Margaret Thatcher

She sounded like the Book of Revelations read out over a railway station public address system by a headmistress of a certain age wearing calico knickers.

—Clive James on Margaret Thatcher

The Prime Minister tells us she has given the French president a piece of her mind, not a gift I would receive with alacrity.

—Denis Healy on Margaret Thatcher

Benjamin Disraeli

A smattering of insults from the ascerbic British Prime Minister:

He has committed every crime that does not require courage.

—on Irish political figure Daniel O'Connell

The right honourable gentleman is reminiscent of a poker. The only difference is that a poker gives off the occasional signs of warmth.

—on Prime Minister Robert Peel

The right honourable gentlemen's smile is like the silver fittings of a coffin.

—also on Robert Peel

If a traveler were informed that such a man was leader of the House of Commons, he may well begin to comprehend how the Egyptians worshipped an insect.

—on Prime Minister Lord John Russell

D I S R A E L I

Inebriated with the exuberance of his own verbosity, and gifted with an egotistical imagination.

—on political opponent Prime Minister William Gladstone

If Mr. Gladstone fell into the Thames, that would be a misfortune; if someone pulled him out, that would be a calamity.

—asked to distinguish between a misfortune and a calamity

He made his conscience not his guide, but his accomplice.

—and again on William Gladstone

VIII.

U.S. Presidents

White House Wit and Vitriol

If ever a nation was debauched by a man, the American nation has been debauched by [him]. If ever a nation was deceived by a man, the American nation was deceived by [him].

—Philadelphia Aurora *on George Washington*

First in peace, first in war, but middle of the pack when it came to humor.

—Bob Dole on George Washington

. . . and as to you, sir, treacherous in private friendship . . . and a hypocrite in public life, the world will be puzzled to decide whether you are an apostate or an imposter, whether you have abandoned good principles, or whether you ever had?

—Thomas Paine to George Washington

It has been the political career of this man to begin with hypocrisy, proceed with arrogance, and finish with contempt.

—Thomas Paine on John Adams

Often cranky and full of insults—an eighteenth-century Don Rickles.

—Bob Dole on John Adams

He is vain, irritable, and a bad calculator of the force and probable effect of the motives which govern men.

—Thomas Jefferson on John Adams

His Rotundity.

—said of John Adams

The moral character of Jefferson was repulsive. Continually puling about liberty, equality and the degrading curse of slavery, he brought his own children to the hammer, and money of his debaucheries.

—*Alexander Hamilton*

. . . Murder, robbery, rape, adultery and incest will be openly taught and practiced, the air will be rent with the cries of distress, the soil soaked with blood, and the nation black with crimes. Where is the heart that can contemplate such a scene without shivering with horror?

—The New England Courant *on the election of Thomas Jefferson*

. . . as for Jemmy Madison—ah! Poor Jemmy! He is but a withered little apple-John.

—*Washington Irving on James Madison*

. . . a commonplace man of no great brilliance.

—John and Alice Durant on James Monroe

His disposition is as perverse and mulish as that of his father.

—James Buchanan on John Quincy Adams

His face is livid, gaunt his whole body, his breath is green with gall; his tongue drips poison.

—John Quincy Adams on a political opponent

A barbarian who could not write a sentence of grammar and hardly could spell his own name.

—John Quincy Adams on Andrew Jackson

He is ignorant, passionate, hypocritical, corrupt and easily swayed by the basest men who surround him.

—Henry Clay on Andrew Jackson

He is certainly the basest, meanest scoundrel that ever disgraced the image of God, nothing is too mean or low for him to condescend to.

—Andrew Jackson on Henry Clay

I didn't shoot Henry Clay and I didn't hang John Calhoun.

—Andrew Jackson, commenting on things he had left undone

Van Buren struts and swaggers like a crow in the gutter. He is laced up in corsets. . . . It would be difficult to say, from his personal appearance, whether he was a man or a woman.

—*U. S. Representative Davy Crockett on Martin Van Buren*

Our Present Imbecile Chief.

—*Andrew Jackson on William Henry Harrison*

. . . a disgusting man to do business with. Coarse, dirty and clownish.

—*William Henry Harrison on John Quincy Adams*

Turnacoat Tyler.

—*his political enemies on John Tyler*

Who is Polk?

—*Whig reaction when the Democrats announced the presidential nomination of James K. Polk*

He was the least conspicuous man who was had ever been nominated for president.

—*Carl R. Fisher on James K. Polk*

He is a bewildered, confounded, and miserably perplexed man.

—*Abraham Lincoln on James K. Polk*

Zachary Taylor's name seems more likely to appear as a *Jeopardy!* question than on any list of presidential greats.

—*historian Catherine Clinton*

. . . a funny-sounding, obscure, mid-nineteenth century president.

—Clinton joke writer Mark Katz on Millard Fillmore

Don't get me wrong. Fillmore's been good for many a chuckle over the years. It's just that most of the laughter has come at his expense.

—Bob Dole

He was another one that was a complete fizzle . . . Pierce didn't know what was going on, and even if he had, he wouldn't of known what to do about it.

—Harry Truman on Franklin Pierce

. . . a bloated mass of political putridity.

—Thaddeus Stevens on James Buchanan

I have just read your dispatch about sore-tongued and fatigued horses. Will you pardon me for asking what the horses of your army have done since the battle of Antietam that fatigues anything?
—Abraham Lincoln in a telegram to General George B. McClellan

The President is nothing more than a well-meaning baboon . . . I went to the White House directly after tea where I found the original Gorilla about as intelligent as ever. What a specimen to be at the head of our affairs now!
—General George McClellan on Abraham Lincoln

My dear McClellan: If you don't want to use the army I should like to borrow it for a while. Yours respectfully, A. Lincoln.
—Abraham Lincoln to General George B. McClellan

Filthy Story-Teller, Despot, Liar, Thief, Braggart, Buffoon, Usurper, Monster, Ignoramus Abe, Old Scoundrel, Perjurer, Robber, Swindler, Tyrant, Field-Butcher, Land Pirate.

—Harper's Weekly *on Abraham Lincoln*

Mr. Lincoln evidently knows nothing of . . . the higher elements of human nature . . . His soul seems made of leather, and incapable of any grand or noble emotion. Compared with the mass of men, he is a line of flat prose in a beautiful and spirited lyric. He lowers, he never elevates you. . . . When he hits upon a policy, substantially good in itself, he contrives to belittle it, besmear it in some way to render it mean, contemptible and useless. Even wisdom from him seems but folly.

—The New York Post

. . . We did not conceive it possible that even Mr. Lincoln would produce a paper so slipshod, so loose-joined, so puerile, not alone in literary construction, but in its ideas, its sentiments, its grasp. He has outdone himself. He has literally come out of the little end of his own horn. By the side of it, mediocrity is superb.

—The Chicago Times *commenting on the Gettysburg Address*

He is such an infernal liar.

—*Ulysses S. Grant on Andrew Johnson*

Grant the Butcher.

—*Civil war nickname of Ulysses S. Grant*

. . . a short, round-shouldered man, in a very tarnished uniform . . . no station, no manner . . . and a rather scrubby look withal.

—*Richard Dana Gibson on Ulysses S. Grant*

His Fraudulency.

—*Democratic nickname for Rutherford B. Hayes*

Rutherfraud.

—*another Democratic nickname*

Garfield has shown that he is not possessed of the backbone of an angleworm.

—*Ulysses S. Grant on James Garfield*

. . . a non-entity with side whiskers . . .

—Woodrow Wilson on Chester A. Arthur

Ma, Ma, where's my Pa? Going to the White House! Ha Ha Ha!

—newspaper rhyme from the Republican claim that Grover Cleveland had fathered an illegitimate child while he was still governor of New York

How could anyone but a moron be glad that he voted for Cleveland?

—Judge after Cleveland's reelection

He is a cold-blooded, narrow-minded, prejudiced, obstinate, timid old psalm-singing Indianapolis politician.

—*Theodore Roosevelt on Benjamin Harrison*

Why, if a man were to call my dog McKinley, and the brute failed to resent to the death the . . . insult, I'd drown it.

—*William Cowper Brann on William E. McKinley*

He has no more backbone than a chocolate eclair.

—*Theodore Roosevelt on William E. McKinley*

I am told he no sooner thinks than he talks, which is a miracle not wholly in accord with an educational theory of forming an opinion.

—*Woodrow Wilson on Theodore Roosevelt*

My father always wanted to be the corpse at every funeral, the bride at every wedding, and the baby at every christening.

—*Alice Roosevelt Longworth on Theodore Roosevelt*

An old maid with testosterone poisoning.

—*Patricia O'Tolle on Theodore Roosevelt*

He is the most dangerous man of the age.

—*Woodrow Wilson on Theodore Roosevelt*

. . . a flub-dub with a streak of the second-rate and the common in him.

—*Theodore Roosevelt on William Howard Taft*

I regard him as a ruthless hypocrite and as an opportunist, who has not convictions he would not barter at once for votes.

—William Howard Taft on Woodrow Wilson

Byzantine logothete.

—Theodore Roosevelt on Woodrow Wilson (the phrase means a glorified accountant)

. . . infernal skunk in the White House.

—Theodore Roosevelt on Woodrow Wilson

Mr. Wilson bores me with his Fourteen Points; why, God Almighty has only ten.

—Georges Clemenceau on Woodrow Wilson

That is to say, he writes the worst English that I have ever encountered. It reminds me of a string of wet sponges; it reminds me of tattered washing on the line; it reminds me of stale bean soup, of college yells, of dogs barking idiotically through endless nights. It is so bad that a sort of grandeur creeps into it. It drags itself out of the dark abysm of pish, and crawls insanely up the topmost pinnacle of posh. It is rumble and bumble. It is flap and doodle. It is balder and dash.

—H. L. Mencken on Warren G. Harding

His speeches leave the impression of an army of pompous phrases moving over the landscape in search of an idea.

—Senator William McAdoo on Warren Harding

. . . the only man woman, or child who wrote a simple declarative sentence with seven grammatical errors is dead.

—e e cummings on Warren Harding

He looks as though he's been weaned on a pickle.

—Alice Roosevelt Longworth on Calvin Coolidge

How can they tell?

—Dorothy Parker, learning of Calvin Coolidge's death

That man has offered me unsolicited advice for six years, all of it bad.

—Calvin Coolidge on Herbert Hoover

He wouldn't commit himself to the time of day from a hatful of watches.

—Westbrook Pegler on Herbert Hoover

Such a little man could not have made so big a depression.

—Norman Thomas on Herbert Hoover

. . . chameleon on plaid.

—Herbert Hoover on Franklin D. Roosevelt

If he became convinced tomorrow that coming out for cannibalism would get him the votes he sorely needs, he would begin fattening a missionary in the White House backyard come Wednesday.

—H. L. Mencken on Franklin D. Roosevelt

To err is Truman.

—A popular joke in 1948

Ike didn't know anything, and all the time he was in office, he didn't learn a thing. . . . The general doesn't know any more about politics than a pig knows about Sunday.

—Harry Truman on Dwight D. Eisenhower

You can always tell a Harvard man but you can't tell him much.

—Dwight Eisenhower on John F. Kennedy (the line did not originate with Eisenhower)

The enviably attractive nephew who sings an Irish ballad for the company and then winsomely disappears before the table clearing and dishwashing begin.

—Lyndon B. Johnson on JFK

He turned out to be so many different characters he could have populated all of War and Peace and still had a few people left over.

—Herbert Mitgang about Lyndon B. Johnson

He inherited some good instincts from his Quaker forebears, but by diligent hard work, he overcame them.

—James Reston on Richard Nixon

He can lie out of both sides of his mouth at the same time, and if he ever caught himself telling the truth, he'd lie just to keep his hand in.

—Harry Truman on Richard Nixon

Avoid all needle drugs. The only dope worth shooting is Richard Nixon.

—*Abbie Hoffman*

He's a nice guy, but he played too much football with his helmet off.

—*Lyndon B. Johnson on Gerald Ford*

History buffs probably noted the reunion at a Washington party a few weeks ago of three ex-presidents: Carter, Ford, and Nixon—See No Evil, Hear No Evil, and Evil.

—*Bob Dole, in a 1983 speech*

A triumph of the embalmer's art.

—*Gore Vidal on Ronald Reagan*

He's proof that there's life after death.

—Mort Sahl on Ronald Reagan

I believe that Ronald Reagan can make this country what it once was—an Arctic region covered with ice.

—Steve Martin

Ronald Reagan doesn't dye his hair, he's just prematurely orange.

—Gerald Ford on Ronald Reagan

I think Nancy does most of his talking; you'll notice that she never drinks water when Ronnie speaks.

—*Robin Williams about Ronald Reagan*

Washington could not tell a lie; Nixon could not tell the truth; Reagan cannot tell the difference.

—*Mort Sahl*

I have been disappointed in almost everything he has done.

—*Jimmy Carter on George H. W. Bush*

When I was president, I said I was a Ford, not a Lincoln. Well, what we have now is a convertible Dodge.

—Gerald Ford on Bill Clinton

I have never seen . . . so slippery, so disgusting a candidate.

—Nat Hentoff talking about Bill Clinton

I wouldn't want any unneutered Clintons in my house.

—former Labor Secretary nominee Linda Chavez, speculating on the reproductive status of the Clintons' cat, Socks

Hell, if you work for Bill Clinton, you go up and down more times than a whore's nightgown.

—*White House advisor James Carville*

What is his accomplishment? That he's no longer an obnoxious drunk?

—*Ron Reagan Jr. on George W. Bush*

He can't help it—he was born with a silver foot in his mouth.

—*former Texas governor Ann Richards on George W. Bush*

Logically unsound, confused and unprincipled, unwise to the extreme.

—Chinese president Jiang Zemin on George W. Bush

If ignorance ever goes to $40 a barrel, I want drilling rights on George Bush's head.

—critic and commentator Jim Hightower on George W. Bush

Calling George Bush shallow is like calling a dwarf short.

—columnist Molly Ivins on George W. Bush

Hopefully, he is not as stupid as he seems, nor as Mafia-like as his predecessors were.

—Fidel Castro on George W. Bush

This guy's as bright as an egg timer.

—Chevy Chase on George W. Bush

Bush is smart. I don't think that Bush will ever be impeached, 'cause unlike Clinton, Reagan, or even his father, George W. is immune from scandal. Because, if George W. testifies that he had no idea what was going on, wouldn't you believe him?

—Jay Leno

Bush/Cheney '04: Putting the "Con" in Conservative.

—*campaign bumper sticker*

Bush the younger has two things going for him that his father never had. One: an easy charm with regular people and two: the power to make them disappear without a trial.

—*Bill Maher*

President Bush is going to establish elections there in Iraq. He's going to rebuild the infrastructure. He's going to create jobs. He said if it works there, he'll try it here.

—*David Letterman*

IX.

Snappy Comebacks

Taut Retorts

John Wilkes was an eighteenth-century English politician of radical leanings. The Earl of Sandwich, a staunch conservative with opposing views, became so irate at something Wilkes said that he exploded, "Egad sir, I do not know whether you will die on the gallows or of the pox."

To which John Wilkes replied, "That will depend, my Lord, on whether I embrace your principles or your mistress."

No danger. For no man in England would take away my life to make you king.

—*King Charles II to his brother the Duke of York after the duke warned him of the danger of traveling unprotected*

When John Wilmot, Earl of Rochester, suggested to King Charles II that his epitaph might be, "Here lies our sovereign lord, the king, Whose word no man relies on, Who never said a foolish thing, And never did a wise one," the king replied, "That is very true, for my words are my own, but my actions are my ministers."

An English duke, annoyed by the slow service at his London club, called a waiter over and harrumphed, "Do you know who I am?"

The waiter replied coolly, "No, sir, I do not. But I shall make inquiries and inform you directly."

New York City lawyer Joseph Choate once opposed a lawyer at a court in Westchester County, a residential area north of the city. In an effort to mock him, the opponent cautioned the jury not to be taken in by Choate's "Chesterfieldian urbanity."

When his turn to sum up came, Choate countered by urging the jury not to be taken in by the other lawyer's "Westchesterfieldian suburbanity."

While traveling by train, *New York Tribune* publisher Horace Greeley noticed a fellow passenger reading the rival *Sun* and asked why he did not read the *Tribune*.

"I take the *Tribune* too," the man replied. "I use it to wipe my arse with."

"Keep it up," Greeley declared, "and eventually you'll have more brains in your arse than you have in your head."

George S. Kaufman said to fellow Algonquin Round Table wit, Marc Connolly, "I like your bald head, Marc. It feels just like my wife's behind."

Connolly replied, feeling his pate, "So it does, George!"

Pompous young man: I can't bear fools.

Dorothy Parker: Apparently, your mother could.

At a dinner party thrown by the producer Arthur Hornblow and his wife, the quite elderly Mrs. Hornblow never stopped talking about her brief theatrical career. When she said for the umpteenth time "Well, when I was on the stage . . ."

Dorothy Parker turned to her dinner companion and said in a loud whisper, "Nonsense, in those days, boys played all the women's parts!"

Clare Booth Luce stood aside and gestured Dorothy Parker to precede her through the door, saying "Age before beauty."

Parker swept on, saying only: "Pearls before swine."

"I suppose life can never get entirely dull to an American, because whenever he can't strike up any other way to put in his time he can always get away with a few years trying to find out who his grandfather was," said Paul Bourget to Mark Twain

"Right, your Excellency. But I reckon a Frenchman's got his little stand-by for a dull time, too; because when all other interests fail he can turn in and see if he can't find out who his father was," Twain replied.

When Mark Twain finished giving one of his customary after-dinner speeches, a prominent lawyer stood up, shoved his hands in his pockets, and said, "Doesn't it strike this company as unusual that a professional humorist should be so funny?"

Twain replied, "Doesn't it strike this company as unusual that a lawyer should have both hands in his own pockets?"

A political rally heckler to presidential candidate Al Smith: Go ahead Al. Tell 'em all you know it won't take long.

Smith: "I'll tell 'em all we both know. It won't take any longer."

Yes, I am a Jew and when the ancestors of the right honourable gentleman were brutal savages in an unknown island, mine were priests in the temple of Solomon.

—Benjamin Disraeli, responding to Member of Parliament Daniel O'Connell's disparaging Disraeli's Jewish ancestry

The violinist Jacques Thibault was handed an autograph book after a concert. "There's not much room on this page," he told his fan. "What shall I write?"

Another violinist standing nearby suggested, "Write your repertoire."

At a dinner party one evening, the movie director Alfred Hitchcock, whose hefty profile betrayed a fondness for food, was dismayed to find that the portions being served were on the meager side.

At the end of the evening, the hostess bid Hitchcock farewell. "I do hope you will dine with us again soon," she added.

"By all means," Hitchcock replied. "Let's start now."

Anonymous actress to Ilka Chase: I enjoyed reading your book [entitled *Past Imperfect*]. Who wrote it for you?

Ilka Chase: Darling, I'm so glad that you liked it. Who read it to you?

Anonymous singer: You know, my dear, I insured my voice for fifty thousand dollars.

Miriam Hopkins: That's wonderful. And what did you do with the money?

As Oscar Wilde took a curtain call at one of his plays that was less than well received, he took the occasion to harangue the audience for their insensitivity to art. "You are Philistines who have invaded this sacred sanctum," he told them.

"And," shouted a voice from the audience, "you are driving us forth with the jawbone of an ass."

Lewis Morris: It is a conspiracy of silence against me—a conspiracy of silence. What should I do?

Oscar Wilde: Join it.

Oscar Wilde: "I wish I had said that."

James McNeill Whistler: "You will, Oscar; you will."

At a party one evening the painter James McNeill Whistler found himself cornered by a notorious bore. "You know, Mr. Whistler," the bore said, "I passed your house last night.

"Thank you," Whistler replied.

Frederic Leighton: My dear Whistler, you leave your pictures in such a sketchy, unfinished state. Why don't you ever finish them?

Whistler: My dear Leighton, why do you ever begin yours?

When the artist James McNeill Whistler's poodle developed a throat infection, Whistler sent immediately for England's leading ear, nose, and throat specialist, Sir Morell Mackenzie. The doctor was not amused when he saw that the patient was a dog, but he conducted a thorough examination, wrote out a prescription, and left with his fee.

The next day Whistler received a message asking him to call on Mackenzie without delay. Fearing some consequences of his dog's illness, Whistler hurried to the doctor's house. "So good of you to come, Mr. Whistler," said Mackenzie, "I wanted to see about painting my front door."

Noel Coward was informed that a certain dim-witted theater manager had shot himself in the head. Coward replied, "he must have been a marvelously good shot."

Noel Coward to Edna Ferber, who was wearing a tailored suit: You look almost like a man.

Edna Ferber: So do you.

The debut performance of George Bernard Shaw's *Arms And The Man* was a great success, but as the playwright took a curtain call, he was interrupted by a solitary hiss from the gallery.

Shaw, raising a hand to silence the crowd, bowed deeply in the heckler's direction. "I quite agree with you, sir," he nodded, "but what can two do against so many?"

The dancer Isadora Duncan wrote to George Bernard Shaw: "You have the greatest brain in the world, and I have the most beautiful body; so we ought to produce the most perfect child."

Shaw replied, "But what if the child inherits my body and your brain?"

When the heavyset G. K. Chesterton, said, "I see there has been a famine in the land," the thin George Bernard Shaw answered, "And I see the cause of it. If I were as fat as you, I would hang myself."

Chesterton replied, "If I were to hang myself, I would use you for the rope."

George Bernard Shaw sent Winston Churchill two tickets for the first night of one of his plays with a note saying: "Bring a friend—if you have one."

Churchill returned the tickets saying he would not be able to attend but would be grateful for tickets for the second night—"if there is one."

An elderly dowager told a young Winston Churchill, "There are two things I don't like about you, Mr. Churchill—your politics and your mustache."

Churchill replied, "My dear madam, pray do not disturb yourself. You are not likely to come into contact with either."

Toward the end of Winston Churchill's life, a member of Parliament remarked when he saw Churchill visiting the House of Commons, "they say he's potty."

Churchill overheard and replied, "they say he can't hear either."

Society grande dame to Winston Churchill: Winston, you're drunk.

Churchill: And you, madam, are ugly. But I shall be sober in the morning.

Lady Astor to Winston Churchill: Mr. Churchill, if you were my husband, I'd put poison in your tea.

Churchill: Madam, if you were my wife . . . I'd drink it.

After dinner one evening a rancher's wife was entertaining their house guest by playing the piano. At one point she turned to the visitor and said, "I understand you love music."

"Yes," murmured the guest politely. "But never you mind. Keep right on playing."

An actor in one of the Gilbert and Sullivan operettas told librettist William S. Gilbert, "See here, sir, I will not be bullied—I know my lines."

To which Gilbert replied, "Possibly, but you don't know mine."

He doesn't have to worry. He'll never be either.

—*Congressman Joseph Reed, after Senator Henry Clay announced "I would rather be right than be president."*

Henry Clay, senator from Kentucky, was sitting on the porch of a Washington, D.C. hotel with Daniel Webster, senator from Massachusetts. As a man leading a tram of mules walked by, Webster commented, "Clay, there go a number of your Kentucky constituents."

Clay replied, "They must be going up to Massachusetts to teach school."

John Randolph, meeting political rival Henry Clay on a narrow sidewalk: I, sir, do not step aside for a scoundrel.

Clay: I, on the other hand, always do.

British playwright Samuel Foote once asked a man why he continuously sang a particular song. "Because it haunts me," the man explained.

"No wonder," Foote replied, "since you are forever murdering it!"

Invited to attend an orgy in Paris, Voltaire accepted with pleasure. The next day, after reporting to his friends that he had enjoyed the experience, he was invited to attend again that evening.

"Ah no, my good friends," he declined, "once a philosopher, twice a pervert."

Right before a Christmas vacation, William Lyons Phelps, professor of literature at Yale University, marked an examination paper on which was written, "God only knows the answer to this question. Merry Christmas."

Phelps returned the exam with "God gets an A. You get an F. Happy New Year."

A young actress was once invited by Ethel Barrymore to dinner—and not only failed to appear but neglected to apologize or account for her absence. A few days later, the two women unexpectedly met. "I think I was invited to your house to dinner last Thursday night," the young woman began.

"Oh, yes?" Barrymore replied. "Did you come?"

One evening George Jessel arrived at the exclusive Stork Club with the black singer and actress Lena Horne on his arm. Sherman Billingsley, the club's owner, and his headwaiters, while hardly ardent supporters of racial equality, nevertheless treated Jessel, a regular customer, with miminal respect.

The headwaiter looked through his reservation book and pretended that there were no openings. "Mr. Jessel," he finally said, "who made the reservation?"

Jessel replied, "Abraham Lincoln."

Arriving at church one Sunday, Henry Ward Beecher found in his mailbox a letter that contained the single word: "Fool."

During the service that morning, he related the incident to his congregation: "I have known many an instance of a man writing a letter and forgetting to sign his name, but this is the only instance I have ever known of a man signing his name and forgetting to write the letter."

When British Labour Party figure Herbert Morrison remarked that he was his own worst enemy, his rival Ernest Bevin immediately replied, "Not while I'm alive, he ain't."

The drama critic James Agate once approached actress Lilian Braithwaite with "My dear lady, may I tell you something I have wanted to tell you for years: that you are the second most beautiful woman in the United Kingdom."

Braithwaite replied, "Thank you, I shall always cherish that as coming from the second-best drama critic." (History does not reveal whom Agate would have named as the first.)

A Harvard man and a Yale man finished at adjoining urinals. The Harvard man proceeded to the sink to wash his hands, while the Yale man went directly to the bathroom door.

The Harvard man said, "At Harvard they teach us to wash our hands after we urinate."

The Yale man replied, "At Yale they teach us not to piss on our hands."

While delivering a campaign speech one day, Theodore Roosevelt was interrupted by a heckler: "I'm a Democrat!" the man shouted. "May I ask the gentleman," Roosevelt replied, quieting the crowd, "why he is a Democrat?"

"My grandfather was a Democrat," the man replied, "my father was a Democrat and I am a Democrat."

"My friend," Roosevelt interjected, "suppose your grandfather had been a jackass and your father was a jackass. What would you then be?"

The heckler replied, "A Republican!"

Calvin Coolidge, who was widely known for being miserly with his speech, was approached by a woman who told him, "Mr. President, I bet my friend that I could get you to say three words to me."

Coolidge replied, "You lose."

When Coolidge and his wife were touring a chicken farm, the foreman noted the sexual prowess of his prize rooster. "Did you know," he said, "that a rooster can provide his services all day without stopping?"

"Ah," said Mrs. Coolidge, "You must tell that to my husband."

Coolidge asked the foreman. "And with the same partner?"

"Oh no," said the foreman, "always with different chickens."

Coolidge replied, "You must tell that to my wife.

The flamboyant Polish pianist Ignace Paderewski was approached in Boston by a bootblack who asked whether he wanted a shoeshine. Paderewski looked down at the boy's dirty face. "No, but if you will wash your face, I will give you a quarter."

The boy ran to a nearby fountain and cleaned himself up, whereupon Paderewski offered him a quarter. The boy briefly admired it, and then returned it: "Keep it, mister," he said, "and get yourself a haircut."

A drunk stumbled up to Groucho Marx, slapped him on the back, and said, "You old son-of-a-gun, you probably don't remember me . . ."

"I never forget a face," Marx replied, "but in your case I'll be glad to make an exception."

Nazi official Hermann Goering collided with an Italian nobleman on a crowded Rome train platform. When the Italian demanded an apology, Goering snapped, "I am Hermann Goering."

"As an excuse that is not enough," the nobleman replied, "but as an explanation it is ample."

Ulysses S. Grant once entered an inn on a stormy winter's night. A number of lawyers in town for a court session were clustered around the fire. One looked up and said, "Here's a stranger, gentlemen, and by the looks of him he's traveled through hell itself to get here."

"That's right," Grant admitted.

"And how did you find things down there?" he was asked.

"Just like here," replied Grant, "the lawyers were all closest to the fire."

"I've been called worse things by better men."

—former Canadian Prime Minister Pierre Trudeau, hearing that Richard Nixon called him "an asshole"

A policeman coming across a young man in a pumpkin patch having "relations" with one of the crop: "Excuse me sir, but do you realize that you are screwing a pumpkin?"

Young man: "A pumpkin?—is it after midnight already?"

Snappy Comebacks to Pick-Up Lines

"Haven't we met before?"

"Yes, I'm the receptionist at the VD Clinic."

"Haven't I seen you someplace before?"

"Yeah, that's why I don't go there anymore."

"Is this seat empty?"

"Yes, and mine will be too if you sit down."

"So, wanna go back to my place?"

"Well, I don't know. Will two people fit under a rock?"

"Your place or mine?"

"Both. You go to yours and I'll go to mine."

"I'd like to call you. What's your number?"
"It's in the phone book."
"But I don't know your name."
"That's in the phone book too."

"What sign were you born under?"
"No Parking."

"Hey, baby, what's your sign?"
"Do Not Enter"

"How do you like your eggs in the morning?"
"Unfertilized!"

"I know how to please a woman."
"Then please leave me alone."

"I want to give myself to you."
"Sorry, I don't accept cheap gifts."

"I can tell that you want me."
"Ohhhh. You're so right. I want you to leave."

"If I could see you naked, I'd die happy."
"Yeah, but if I saw you naked, I'd probably die laughing."

"Your body is like a temple."
"Sorry, there are no services today."

"I'd go through anything for you."
"Good! Let's start with your bank account."

"I would go to the end of the world for you."
"Yes, but would you stay there?"

Snappy Comebacks to "Why aren't you married yet?"

I was hoping to do something meaningful with my life.

What? And spoil my great sex life?

Nobody would believe me wearing white.

Because I just love hearing this question.

It gives my mother something to live for.

My fiancé is waiting for his (or her) parole.

I'm still hoping for a shot at Miss America.

Do you know how hard it is to get two tickets to Miss Saigon?

I'm waiting until I get to be your age.

It didn't seem worth a blood test.

I already have enough laundry to do, thank you.

Because I think it would take all the spontaneity out of dating.

My co-op board doesn't allow spouses.

They just opened a great singles bar on my block.

I wouldn't want my parents to drop dead from sheer happiness.

What? And lose all the money I've invested in running personal ads?

I don't want to have to support another person on my paycheck.

Why aren't you thin?

I'm married to my career, although recently we have been considering a trial separation.

Snappy Comebacks when a Patient in the Hospital

And how are we this morning?

Judging by the way I feel and the way you look, I'd say we're both in trouble.

I know someone who had the very same thing last year, and today he's fine!

That was me—and I got it again.

We'll have you up and around before you know it.

And probably before I'm ready.

I just dropped by! I can only stay a minute.

I'll start the timer now.

If there's anything you want, don't hesitate to ask.

Okay—shut the door from the outside.

X.

SHAKESPEARE

The Unkindest Cuts of All

Before we turn to the Bard's Greatest Insults, here are five dissenting views of Will's works:

The players have often mentioned it as an honour to Shakespeare that, in his writing, whatsoever is penned, he never blotted out a line. My answer hath been "Would that he have blotted a thousand."

—*Ben Johnson*

It is a vulgar and barbarous drama . . . one would imagine this piece to be the work of a drunken savage.

—*Voltaire on Shakespeare's* Hamlet

Never did any author precipitate himself from such heights of thought to so low expressions, as he often does. He is the very Janus of poets; he wears, almost everywhere, two faces: and you have scarce begun to admire the one, e'er you despise the other.

—*John Dryden*

I am more easily bored with Shakespeare and have suffered more ghastly evenings with Shakespeare than with any other dramatist I know.

—*Peter Brook*

It would be positive relief to dig him up and throw stones at him.

—*George Bernard Shaw*

You would answer very well to a whipping.

Scurvy, old, filthy, scurvy lord.

Methink thou art a general offence, and every man should beat thee.

Your virginity breeds mites, much like a cheese.

You are not worth another word, else I'd call you knave.

The complaints I have heard of you I do not all believe; 'tis my slowness that I do not, for I know you lack not folly to commit them and have ability enough to make such knaveries yours.

She is too mean to have her name repeated.

He's a most notable coward, an infinite and endless liar, an hourly promise breaker, the owner of not one good quality.

Drunkenness is his best virtue, for he will be swine drunk, and in his sleep he does little harm, save to his bedclothes about him.

He excels his brother for a coward, yet his brother is reputed one of the best there is. In a retreat, he outruns any lackey.

He looks like a poor, decayed, ingenious, foolish, rascally knave.

I saw the man today, if man he be.

—*All's Well that Ends Well*

Pray you, stand farther from me.

Die a beggar.

Thou didst drink the stale of horses and the guilded puddle which beasts would cough at.

O slave, of no more trust than love that's hir'd.

Slave, soulless villain, dog! O rarely base!

—*Antony and Cleopatra*

What shall I call thee when thou art a man?

Sweep on, you fat and greasy citizens.

I think he be transformed into a beast; for I can nowhere find him like a man.

And in his brain,—which is as dry as the remainder biscuit after a voyage,—he hath strange places cramm'd.

Let's meet as little as we can.

I desire that we be better strangers.

I was seeking for a fool when I found you.

His kisses are Judas's own children.

You lisp and wear strange suits.

—*As You Like It*

If thou art changed to aught, 'tis to an ass.

She's the kitchen wench, and all grease; and I know not what use to put her but to make a lamp of her and run her from her own light. I warrant, her rags and the tallow in them will burn a Poland winter. If she lives till doomsday, she'll burn a week longer than the whole world.

Her complexion is like Swart, like my shoe, but her face nothing like so clean kept, for why, she sweats, a man may go over shoes in the grime of it.

No longer from head to foot than from hip to hip, she is spherical, like a globe, I could find out countries in her.

He is deformed, crooked, old and sere, ill-faced, worse bodied, shapeless everywhere, vicious, ungentle, foolish, blunt, unkind, stigmatical in making, worse in mind.

—*The Comedy of Errors*

What's the matter you dissentious rogue that, rubbing the poor itch of your opinion, make yourselves scabs?

Boils and plagues plaster you over, that you may be abhorred farther than seen and one infect another against the wind a mile. You souls of geese that bear the shapes of men.

I find the ass in compound with the major part of your syllables.

Priests must become mockers, if they shall encounter such ridiculous subjects as you.

Your beards deserve not so honourable a grave as to stuff a botcher's cushion or to be entombed in an ass's pack saddle.

More of your conversation would infect my brain.

He's a disease that must be cut away.

You are the must chaff, and you are smelt above the moon.

The tartness of his face sours ripe grapes, when he walks he moves like an engine and the ground shrinks before his treading.

—*Coriolanus*

As I told you always, her beauty and her brain go not together.

A wholesome jackanapes must take me up for swearing, as if I borrowed mine oaths of him.

Thy tongue outvenoms all the worms of Nile.

This Cloten was a fool, an empty purse, there was no money in it. Not Hercules could have knocked out his brains for he had none.

—*Cymbeline*

What such fellows as I do, crawling between earth and heaven? We are arrant knaves all, believe none of us.

If thou dost marry, I'll give thee this plague for thy dowry, be thou as chaste as ice, as pure as snow, thou shall not escape calumny.

It offends me to the soul to hear a robustious periwig pated fellow tear a passion to tatters, to very rags.

Thou are pigeon-liver'd and lack gall.

My two schoolfellows. Whom I shall trust as I will adders' fangs.

—*Hamlet*

I see a good amendment of life in thee, from praying to purse-taking.

Peace, ye fat guts.

There is no more valour in that Poins than in a wild duck.

Falstaff sweats to death and lards the lean earth as he walks along.

Out, you mad headed ape. A weasel hath not such a deal of spleen as you are tossed with.

Why, thou clay brained guts, thou knotty pated fool, thou whoreson obscene greasy tallow catch.

What a slave art thou to hack thy sword as thou hast done, and then say it was in a fight.

Do thou amend thy face, and I'll amend my life.

—*Henry IV, Part I*

Your means are very slender, and your waist is great.

You are as a candle, the better part burnt out.

I scorn you, scurvy companion. What, you poor, base, rascally, cheating, lack-linen mate! Away, you moldy rogue, away!

He hath eaten me out of house and home, he hath put all my substance into that fat belly of his.

What a disgrace it is to me that I should remember your name.

What a maidenly man at arms you have become.

Hang yourself, you muddy conger.

His wit's as thick as a Tewkesbury mustard.

A ruffian that will swear, drink, dance, revel the night, rob, murder and commit the oldest of sins the newest kind of ways.

Thou damned tripe visaged rascal.

You scullion! You rampallian! You fustilarian! I'll tickle your catastrophe!

—Henry IV, Part II

Thou cruel, ingrateful, savage and inhuman creature.

Thine face is not worth sunburning.

Die and be damned.

What a wretched and peevish fellow is this King.

Thou damned and luxurious mountain goat.

He be as good a gentleman as the devil is, as Lucifer and Beelzebub himself.

If I owe you anything I shall pay you in cudgels.

—Henry V

Your hearts I'll stamp out with my horse's heel and make a quagmire of your mingled brains.

Vile fiend and shameless courtesan.

—Henry VI, Part I

He begins a new hell in himself.

All goodness is poison to thy stomach.

—Henry VIII

You have some sick offence within your mind.

—Julius Caesar

You are not worth the dust which the rude wind blows in your face.

A knave, a rascal, an eater of broken meats, a base, proud, shallow, beggarly, three-suited, action-taking, whoreson glass-gazing, superserviceable, finical rogue; one-trunk-inheriting slave; one that wouldst be a bawd in way of good service, and art nothing but the composition of a knave, beggar, coward, pander, and the son and heir of a mongrel bitch, one whom I will beat into clamorous whining if thou deniest the least syllable of thy addition.

—*King Lear*

Fit to govern? No, not fit to live.

The rump-fed ronyon cries.

Go, prick thy face, and over-red thy fear, thou lily-liver'd boy.

Your sole name blisters our tongue.

—*Macbeth*

Thou art a flesh-monger, a fool and a coward.

I pray a thousand prayers for thy death; no words to save thee.

A fool, a coward, one all of luxury, an ass, a madman.

You speak unskilfully: or, if your knowledge be more, it is much darkened in your malice.

—*Measure for Measure*

Gratiano speaks an infinite deal of nothing.

I had rather be married to a death's head with a bone in his mouth.

When he is best, he is a little worse than a man, and when he is worst, he is little better than a beast.

A villain with a smiling cheek, a goodly apple rotten at the heart.

A stony adversary, an inhuman wretch, uncapable of pity, void and empty from any dram of mercy.

Beg that thou may have leave to hang thyself.

—*The Merchant of Venice*

You Banbury cheese.

How now, Mephostophilus?

O base hungarian wight.

Rogues, hence, avant—vanish, like hailstones go.

What tempest, I trow, threw this whale with so many tons of oil in his belly, ashore at Windsor?

The wicked fire of lust have melted him in his own grease.

Ford's a knave, and I will aggravate his style.

King Urinal.

Dishonest varlet, we cannot misuse him enough.

Out of my door, you witch, you hag, you baggage, you polecat, you ronyon!

Vile worm, you were overlooked even in thy birth.

—*The Merry Wives of Windsor*

You cowardly, giant-like ox-beef!

Tempt not too much the hatred of my spirit, for I am sick when I do look on thee.

I do repent the tedious minutes I with her have spent.

What hempen homespun have we swaggering here.

What fools these mortals be.

—*A Midsummer Night's Dream*

Being no other but as she is, I do not like her.

You are duller than a great thaw.

—*Much Ado About Nothing*

You are an index and prologue to the history of lust and foul thoughts.

—*Othello*

Thou art the rudeliest welcome to this world.

He did not flow from honourable sources.

The pox upon her green sickness.

Thou art like the harpy, which, to betray, dost with thine angels face, seize with thine eagle's talons.

Your peevish chastity is not worth a breakfast in the cheapest country.

—*Pericles, Prince of Tyre*

Out of my sight! Thou dost infect my eyes.

A knot you are of damned blood suckers.

Thy mother's name is ominous to children.

Wretched, bloody and usurping boar!

Thou poisonous bunch-back'd toad!

Thou art unfit for any place but hell.

—*Richard III*

A fan to hide her face, for her fan's the fairer face!

He is not the flower of courtesy.

Thy head is as full of quarrels as an egg is full of meat.

You ratcatcher.

—*Romeo and Juliet*

How foul and loathsome is thine image.

Think'st thou, though her father be very rich, any man is so very a fool to be married to hell?

I know she is an irksome brawling scold.

A monster, a very monster in apparel.

Away, you three-inch fool!

You heedless joltheads and unmannered slaves.

—*The Taming of the Shrew*

Does thy other mouth call me?

Thine forward voice, now, is to speak well of thine friend; thine backward voice is to utter foul speeches and to detract.

—*The Tempest*

Thou disease of a friend!

—*Timon of Athens*

Foul spoken coward, that thund'rest with thy tongue, and with thy weapon nothing dares perform.

Why, what a caterwauling dost thou keep!

As loathsome as a toad.

Say wall eyed slave, whither wouldst thou convey this growing image of thy fiend like face?

—*Titus Andronicus*

He has not so much a brain as ear-wax.

—*Troilus and Cressida*

Go shake your ears!

Go to, you're a dry fool, I'll no more of you.

He speaks nothing but madman.

Lady, you are the cruelst she alive.

Observe him, for the love of mockery.

You are now sailed into the north of my ladies opinion, where you will hang like an icicle on a Dutchman's beard.

A fiend like thee might bear my soul to hell.

Leave thy vain bibble-babble.

—*Twelfth Night*

If you spend word for word with me, I shall make your wit bankrupt.

She is peevish, sullen, forward, proud, disobedient, stubborn, lacking duty.

She hath more hair than wit, and more faults than hairs, and more wealth than faults.

—*The Two Gentlemen of Verona*

He makes a July's day short as December.

Female Bastard!

—*The Winter's Tale*

XI.

One-liners

Yo' Mamas and Other Zingers

- Yo' mama is so big, when she sits around the house she sits *around the house*!

- Yo' mama is so fat, when she steps on a scale it says, To Be Continued . . .

- Yo' mama is so ugly, when she worked at the bakery, they dipped her face in the batter to make animal crackers.

- Yo' mama's breath is so nasty that when she burps, her teeth have to duck.

- Yo' mama is so poor, burglars break into her home and leave money.

- Yo' mama is so fat, when she dances the band skips.

- Yo' mama's house is so dirty, the roaches ride around in dune buggies.

- Yo' mama is so ugly, her mama had to tie a pork chop to her neck to make the dog play with her.

- Yo' mama so smelly the government make her wear a Biohazard warning.

- Yo' mama is so fat, she's got more chins than the Hong Kong phone book.

- Yo' mama so stupid she thinks a quarterback is a refund!

- Yo' mama is so ugly, her shadow gave up.

- Yo' mama is so fat, her blood type is Ragu.

- Yo' mama so stupid she could trip over a cordless phone!

- Yo' mama is so ugly, when she was born the Doc smacked her face.

- Yo' mama so stupid, she studied for a drug test!

- Yo' mama is so fat, when she wears her BVDs they spell "Boulevard."

- Yo' mama so stupid, she was born on Independence Day and can't remember her birthday.

- Yo' mama so fat, when her beeper goes off, people think she's backing up.

- Yo' mama so stupid, she bought a solar-powered flashlight!

- Yo' mama and daddy are so poor, they got married for the rice.

- Yo' mama's so big, her belly button's got an echo.

- Yo' mama is so fat that she went outside in a yellow raincoat and people yelled "taxi!"

- Yo' mama's car is so old, they stole "The Club" and left the car.

- Yo' mama is so fat that when God said, "Let there be light," He told her to stand out of the way first.

- Yo' mama is so ugly, your papa takes her to work so he doesn't have to kiss her goodbye.

- Yo' mama is so old that when I told her to act her age, she died.

- Yo' mama is so short, she's got to slam-dunk her bus fare.

- Yo' mama is so fat, when she walked into the all-you-can-eat buffet, they had to install speed bumps.

- Yo' mama so stupid, she sold her car for gasoline money!

- Yo' mama is so fat, when I swerved to avoid her in the street I ran out of gas.

- Yo' mama is so old, she owes Jesus three bucks.

- Yo' mama is so fat, she has to get out of the car to change radio stations.

- Yo' mama's so big, that she climbed Mt. Fuji with one step.

- Yo' mama so stupid it took her two hours to watch *60 Minutes*.

ONE-LINERS

A solemn, unsmiling, sanctimonious old iceberg who looked like he was waiting for a vacancy in the Trinity.

—*Mark Twain*

The only genius with an IQ of 60.

—*Gore Vidal on Andy Warhol*

No woman of our time has gone further with less mental equipment.

—*Clifton Fadiman on Clare Booth Luce*

She looked like a huge ball of fur on two well-developed legs.

—*Nancy Mitford on Princess Margaret*

She's about as feminine as a sidewalk drill.

—*Maryon Allen on Phyllis Schlafly*

I feel so miserable without you, it's almost like having you here.

—*Stephen Bishop*

You're a parasite for sore eyes.

—*Gregory Ratoff*

Sometimes I need what only you can provide: your absence.

—*Ashleigh Brilliant*

There's nothing wrong with you that reincarnation won't cure.

—*Jack E. Leonard*

I'll bet your father spent the first year of your life throwing rocks at the stork.

—*Irving Brecher*

You're a good example of why some animals eat their young.

—*Jim Samuels*

I've just learned about his illness. Let's hope it's nothing trivial.

—*Irvin S. Cobb*

If you ever become a mother, can I have one of the puppies?

—*Charles Pierce*

Pushing forty? She's hanging on for dear life.

—*Dame Ivy Compton-Burnett*

You had to stand in line to hate him.

—*Hedda Hopper*

You have a good and kind soul. It just doesn't match the rest of you.

—*Norm Papernick*

You take the lies out of him, and he'll shrink to the size of your hat; you take the malice out of him, and he'll disappear.

—*Mark Twain*

I never liked him and I always will.

—*Dave Clark*

I like long walks, especially when they are taken by people who annoy me.

—*Fred Allen*

I regard you with an indifference bordering on aversion.

—*Robert Louis Stevenson*

He looked as inconspicuous as a tarantula on a slice of angel food.

—*Raymond Chandler*

He's completely unspoiled by failure.

—*Noel Coward*

His mother should have thrown him away and kept the stork.

—*Mae West*

I could never learn to like her, except on a raft at sea with no other provisions in sight.

—*Mark Twain*

Every time I look at you I get a fierce desire to be lonesome.

—*Oscar Levant*

She was kind of girl who'd eat all your cashews and leave you with nothing but peanuts and filberts.

—*Raymond Chandler*

No one can have a higher opinion of him than I have; and I think he's a dirty little beast.

—*W. S. Gilbert*

You're a mouse studying to be a rat.

—*Wilson Mizner*

The perfection of rottenness.

—*William James*

He was so narrow-minded that if he fell on a pin it would blind him in both eyes.

—*Fred Allen*

He was distinguished for ignorance; for he had only one idea and that was wrong.

—*Benjamin Disraeli*

When I see a man of shallow understanding extravagantly clothed, I feel sorry—for the clothes.

—*Josh Billings*

Why do you sit there looking like an envelope without any address on it?

—*Mark Twain*

Why don't you get a haircut? You look like a chrysanthemum.

—*P. G. Wodehouse*

You couldn't tell if she was dressed for an opera or an operation.

—*Irvin S. Cobb*

A brain of feathers, and a heart of lead.

—*Alexander Pope*

A mental midget with the IQ of a fence post.

—*Tom Waits*

A wit with dunces, and a dunce with wits.

—*Alexander Pope*

Doesn't know much, but leads the league in nostril hair.

—*Josh Billings*

No more sense of direction than a bunch of firecrackers.

—*Rob Wagner*

Stay with me; I want to be alone.

—*Joey Adams*

That young girl is one of the least benightedly unintelligent organic life forms it has been my profound lack of pleasure not to be able to avoid meeting.

—*Douglas Adams*

Useless as a pulled tooth.

—*Mary Roberts Rinehart*

I thought men like that shot themselves.

—*King George V*

While he was not dumber than an ox, he was not any smarter either.

—James Thurber

They say you shouldn't say nothin' about the dead unless it's good. He's dead. Good.

—Moms Mabley

He's got a wonderful head for money. There's this long slit on the top.

—Sir David Frost

When you use your brain it's a violation of the child-labor law.

—Joe E. Lewis

A sophisticated rhetorician, inebriated with the exuberance of his own verbosity.

—*Benjamin Disraeli*

He's a self-made man . . . the living proof of the horrors of unskilled labor!

—*Ed Wynn*

What's on your mind?—if you'll forgive the overstatement.

—*Fred Allen*

She's the sort of woman who lives for others—you can tell the others by their hunted expression.

—*C. S. Lewis*

So boring you fall asleep halfway through her name.

—*Alan Bennett*

She never lets ideas interrupt the easy flow of her conversation.

—*Jean Webster*

She has been kissed as often as a police-court Bible, and by much the same class of people.

—*Robertson Davies*

She is such a good friend that she would throw all her acquaintances into the water for the pleasure of fishing them out again.

—Charles-Maurice de Talleyrand-Perigord

She tells enough white lies to ice a wedding cake.

—Margot Asquith

I'd call him a sadistic, hippophilic necrophile, but that would be beating a dead horse.

—Woody Allen

Selected Quoted Sources

Adams, Douglas (1952–2001), British writer

Adams, Joey (1911–1999), American actor

Adams, John (1735–1826), second U.S. president

Adams, John Quincy (1767–1848), sixth U.S. president

Addison, Joseph (1672–1719), British essayist, poet, statesman

Affleck, Ben (b. 1972), American actor

Agnew, Spiro (1918–1996), thirty-ninth U. S. vice president

Alcott, Louisa May (1832–1888), American novelist

Ali, Muhammad (b. 1942), American prizefighter

Allen, Fred (1894–1956), American radio personality and actor

Allen, Woody (b. 1935), American comedian, actor, and producer

Aristophanes (c. 448–388 B.C.), Athenian playwright

Asquith, Margot (1864–1945), British politician and writer

Astaire, Fred (1899–1987), American dancer and actor

Astor, Lady Nancy (1879–1964), British politician

Auden, W. H. (1907–1973), Anglo-American poet

Austen, Jane (1775–1817), English novelist

Balzac, Honoré de (1799–1850), French writer

Baring, Maurice (1874–1945), British diplomat, journalist, and author

Barkley, Charles (b. 1963), American basketball player

Barrie, Sir James Matthew (1860–1937), British writer

Barry, Dave (b. 1947), American humor columnist

Barrymore, Drew (b. 1975), American actress

Barrymore, Lionel (1878–1954), American stage and film actor

Baudelaire, Charles (1821–1867), French poet and critic

Beecham, Sir Thomas (1879–1961), British orchestral conductor

Beecher, Henry Ward (1813–1837), American clergyman

Beethoven, Ludwig van (1770–1827), German composer

Behan, Brendan (1923–1964), Irish dramatist

Belloc, Hilaire (1870–1953), English author

Benny, Jack (1894–1974), American comedian

Berle, Milton (1908–2002), American television comedian and film actor

Berlioz, Hector (1803–1869), French composer

Bernhard, Sandra (b. 1955), American comedian

Bernhardt, Sarah (1844–1923), French actress

Berry, Chuck (b. 1926), American rock music guitarist, singer, and songwriter

Billings, Josh (1818–1885), American humorous essayist

Birkenhead, F. E. Smith, first Earl of (1872–1930), British politician

Blackwell, Richard, "Mr. Blackwell" (b. 1913), American fashion critic

Bombeck, Erma (1927–1996), author and columnist

Bonaparte, Napoleon (1769–1821), French emperor and general

Borg, Björn (b. 1956), Swedish tennis player

Borge, Victor (1909–2000), Danish-American musical entertainer

Boswell, James (1740–1795), Scottish author

Bowen, Elizabeth (1899–1973), Anglo-Irish novelist

Bowie, David (b. 1947), British rock and roll singer and songwriter

Boy George, stage name of George O. Dowd (b. 1961), British pop singer

Brahms, Johannes (1833–1897), German composer

Braithwaite, Lilian (1873–1948), British actress

Brando, Marlon (1924–2004), American film actor

Brann, William Cowper (1855–1898), American journalist

Breslin, Jimmy (b. 1930), American journalist

Brown, Rita Mae (b. 1944), American author and social activist

Browning, Robert (1812–1889), British poet

Bruce, Lenny (1925–1966), American comedian

Brummel, George Bryan "Beau" (1778–1840), British dandy and wit

Bryan, William Jennings (1860–1925), American lawyer and politician

Bryson, Bill (b. 1951), American writer

Buchanan, James (1791–1868), fifteenth U.S. president

Burns, George (1896–1996), American actor

Burton, Richard (1925–84), British actor

Bush, George H. W. (b. 1924), forty-first U.S. president

Bush, George W. (b. 1946), forty-third U.S. president

Butler, Samuel (1835–1902), British novelist and critic

Byron, George Gordon Noel Byron, sixth Baron (1788–1824), British romantic poet

Cain, James M. (1892–1977), American novelist

Campbell, Mrs. Patrick (1865–1940), English actress

Capote, Truman (1924–1984), American author

Carlyle, Thomas (1795–1881), British historian

Caroline Wilhelmina (1683–1737), Queen Consort of King George II of England

Carson, Johnny (1925–2005), American television host and personality

Carter, Jimmy (b. 1924), thirty-ninth U.S. president

Castro, Fidel (b. 1926), premier of Cuba

Chandler, Raymond (1888–1959), American author

Chase, Chevy (b. 1943), American comedian and actor

Chase, Ilka (1905–1978), American actress and writer

Chesterton, G. K. (1974–1936), British author

Choate, Joseph (1932–1967), American lawyer and diplomat

Chopin, Frederic (1810–1849), Polish composer

Churchill, Sir Winston (1874–1965), British statesman and author

Clay, Henry (1777–1852), American politician

Clemenceau, Georges (1841–1929), French statesman

Clemens, Samuel: see Mark Twain

Coleridge, Samuel Taylor (1772–1834), British romantic poet

Colombo, John (b. c.1936), Canadian author

Compton-Burnett, Dame Ivy (1892–1969), English novelist

Connolly, Cyril (1903–1974), English critic and editor

Connor, William (1909–1967), British journalist under the pen name Cassandra

Conrad, Joseph (1857–1924), British novelist

Constable, John (1776–1837), English painter

Coolidge, Calvin (1872–1933), thirtieth U.S. president

Copland, Aaron (1900–1990), American composer

Cosell, Howard (1920–1995), American sports broadcaster

Coward, Noel (1899–1973), British playwright and composer

Crawford, Joan (1908–1977), American movie star

Crockett, Davy (1786–1836), American frontiersman

cummings, e e (1894–1962), American author

Dangerfield, Rodney (1921–2004), American comedian

Davies, Robertson (b. 1913), Canadian novelist

Davis, Bette (1908–1989), American film actress

Depp, Johnny (b. 1963), American actor

Dickens, Charles (1812–1870), British novelist

Dickey, James (1923–1997), American poet and novelist

Dietrich, Marlene (1901–1992), German-American film actress

Disraeli, Benjamin first Earl of Beaconsfield (1804–1881), British statesman and author

Dole, Bob (b. 1923), U.S. senator

Douglas, Norman (1868–1952), British novelist and essayist

Dowd, Maureen (b. 1952), American newspaper journalist and author

Dreiser, Theodore (1871–1945), American novelist

Dryden, John (1631–1700), British poet laureate

Duncan, Isadora (1878–1927), American dancer

Dykstra, Lillian (1894–1977), American educator and writer

Eisenhower, Dwight David (1890–1969), thirty-fourth U.S. president

Eliot, George (1819–1880), pseudonym of Mary Ann Evans, British novelist

Eliot, T. S. (1885–1968), British poet and winner of the Nobel Prize for Literature

Emerson, Ralph Waldo (1803–1882), American philosopher and poet

Ephron, Nora (b. 1941), American screenwriter, director, and actress

Fadiman, Clifton (1902–1999), literary critic

Faulkner, William, (1897–1962)American author and Nobel Prize winner

Fields, W. C. (1880–1946), American comic actor

Fitzgerald, F. Scott (1896–1940), American novelist

Flaubert, Gustave (1821–1880), French novelist

Foote, Samuel (1720–1777), British playwright

Ford, Ford Madox (1873–1939), English author

Ford, Henry (1863–1947), American industrialist

Fowler, Gene (1890–1960), American journalist

Franklin, Benjamin (1706–1790), American statesman and writer

Frazier, Joe (b. 1944), American heavyweight boxing champion

Freccia, Massimo (1906–2004), Italian conductor and critic

Freud, Sigmund (1856–1939), Austrian psychoanalyst

Frost, Sir David (b. 1939), British television personality

Frost, Robert (1874–1963), American poet

Gallico, Paul (1897–1976), American novelist

Gandhi, Mohandas (1869–1948), Indian political and spiritual leader

Garagiola, Joe (b. 1926), American sportscaster

Gardner, Ava (b. 1922), American actress

Gazzara, Ben (b. 1930), American actor

Gibbon, Edward (1737–1794), British historian

Gielgud, Sir John (1904–2000), English actor

Gleason, Jackie (1916–1987), American actor

Goldsmith, Oliver (c. 1730–1774), British-Irish author and dramatist

Goldwater, Barry (1909–1998), U.S. senator

Gore, Thomas P. (1870–1949), U.S. senator

Grant, Ulysses S. (1822–1885), eighteenth U.S. president

Gray, Thomas (1716–1771), English poet

Greeley, Horace (1811–1872), American newspaper editor

Greene, Graham (1904–1991), English novelist and playwright

Hadas, Moses (1900–1966), American editor

Hamilton, Alexander (1757–1804), American statesman, secretary of the treasury

Hardie, James Keir (1856–1915), British politician

Hardy, Thomas (1840–1928), British novelist

Harris, Richard (b. 1930), Irish actor

Hawthorne, Nathaniel (1804–1864), American writer

Hayes, Helen (1900–1993), American actress

Hecht, Ben (1894–1964), American writer

Heifetz, Jascha (1901–1987), Russian violinist

Hellman, Lillian (1905–1984), American dramatist

Hemingway, Ernest (1899–1961), American writer

Henry, O., pseudonym of William Sydney Porter (1862–1910), American short-story writer

Hepburn, Katharine (1907–2003), American actress

Hitchcock, Alfred (1889–1980), British film director

Hoffman, Abbie (1936–1989), American political activist

Hoover, Herbert (1874–1964), thirty-first U.S. president

Hope, Bob (1903–2003), American radio and television comedian and film actor

Hopkins, Miriam (1902–1972), American actress

Housman, A. E. (1859–1936), English poet and scholar

Howe, Gordie (b. 1928), Canadian hockey player

Howells, William Dean (1837–1920), American novelist, critic, and editor

Hunt, Leigh (1784–1859), English poet

Huxley, Aldous (1894–1963), British novelist

Ickes, Harold (1874–1952), American politician

Idol, Billy (b. 1955), British rock and roll singer

Irving, Washington (1783–1859), American author and diplomat

Ivins, Molly (b. 1944), American journalist

Jackson, Andrew (1767–1845), seventh U.S. president

Jackson, Jesse (b. 1941), American civil rights leader and politician

Jagger, Mick (b. 1943), British lead singer of The Rolling Stones

James, Clive (b. 1939), Australian critic and television personality

James, Henry (1843–1916), American novelist and critic

James, William (1842–1910), American philosopher

Jefferson, Thomas (1743–1826), third U.S. president

Johnson, Andrew (1808–1875), seventeenth U.S. president

Johnson, Ben (1572–1637), English dramatist and poet

Johnson, Lyndon B. (1908–1973), thirty-sixth U.S. president

Johnson, Samuel (1709–1784), English author

Joyce, James (1882–1941), Irish novelist

Kaufman, George S. (1889–1961), American playwright, director, and journalist

Kennedy, John Fitzgerald (1917–1963), thirty-fifth U.S. president

Kerouac, Jack (1922–1969), American novelist

Kierkegaard, Søren (1813–1855), Danish philosopher

Kipling, Rudyard (1865–1936), British and Indian author

Lamb, Lady Caroline (1785–1828), British writer

Lamb, Charles (1775–1834), English essayist

Landor, Walter Savage (1775–1864), British poet

Lardner, Ring (1885–1933), American humorist and short-story writer

Lawrence, D. H. (1885–1930), British novelist

Leno, Jay (b. 1950), American comedian and TV host

Leonard, Hugh, pseudonym of John Keyes Byrne (b. 1926), Irish playwright and author

Letterman, David (b. 1947), television comedian and host

Levant, Oscar (1906–1972), American pianist and wit

Lewis, C. S. (1898–1963), British writer

Liberace, (1919–1987), American pianist and performer

Lincoln, Abraham (1809–1865), sixteenth U.S. president

Longworth, Alice Roosevelt (1884–1980), American political hostess

Lowell, James Russell (1819–1891), American editor and diplomat

Luce, Claire Booth (1903–1987), American editor, playwright, and diplomat

Luther, Martin (1483–1546), German leader of the Protestant Reformation

MacArthur, Douglas (1880–1964), American general

Macaulay, Thomas Babington, first Baron Macaulay (1800–1859), British historian, writer, and politician

Macdonald, Dwight (1906–1982), American author and editor

Mailer, Norman (b. 1923), American writer

Mansfield, Jayne (1933–1967), American actress

Marcus, Greil (b. 1945), American pop music critic

Martin, Billy (1928–1989), New York Yankees manager

Martin, Steve (b. 1945), American comedian, actor, and writer

Marvell, Andrew (1621–1678), British metaphysical poet

Matthau, Walter (1920–2000), American actor

McAdoo, William (1863–1941), American lawyer and politician

McCarthy, Mary (1912–1989), American writer

McCartney, Paul (b. 1942), British singer/songwriter, member of the Beatles

McClellan, General George (1826–1885), American Civil War general

McCullers, Carson (1917–1967), American novelist

McEnroe, John (b. 1959), American tennis player

Melbourne, Henry Lamb, Lord (1749–1848), British politician and diplomat

Mencken, Henry Louis (1880–1956), American editor and critic

Mercer, Johnny (1909–1976), American composer of popular music

Mercury, Freddie (1946–1991), Zanzibar musician and singer

Meredith, George (1828–1909), English novelist and poet

Merman, Ethel (1908–1984), American musical comedy singer

Midler, Bette (b. 1946), American actress

Miller, Henry (1891–1980), American author

Milton, John (1608–1674), British poet

Moore, George (1852–1933), English author

Nash, Ogden (1902–1971), American poet

Nathan, George Jean (1882–1958), American editor and drama critic

Newhart, Bob (b. 1929), American comedian and actor

Nietzsche, Friedrich Wilhelm (1844–1900), German philosopher

Niven, David (1910–1983), Scottish-American actor

O'Neill, Eugene (1888–1953), American dramatist and Nobel Prize winner

O'Rourke, P. J. (b. 1947), American political satirist

Osborne, John (1929–1994), English dramatist

Paar, Jack (1918–2004), American television personality

Paine, Thomas (1737–1809), British-American political activist

Palmer, Jim (b. 1945), American baseball player

Parker, Dorothy (1893–1967), American writer and critic

Pegler, Westbrook (1894–1969), American newspaper columnist

Penn, Sean (b. 1960), American actor

Perelman, S. J. (1904–1979), American humorist and author

Phelps, William Lyon (1865–1943), U.S. educator and literary critic

Pope, Alexander (1688–1744), British poet and satirist

Pound, Ezra (1885–1972), American poet

Preminger, Otto (1906–1986), Austrian director

Priestley, J. B. (1894–1984), English author

Prince (b. 1958), American singer and musician

Quindlen, Anna (b. 1953), American writer

Rabelais, François (c.1490–1553), French writer and physician

Reed, Rex (b. 1938), American film critic and columnist

Reger, Max (1873–1916), German composer

Richards, Ann (b. 1933), American politician

Richards, I. A. (1893–1979), English literary critic

Richards, Keith (b. (1943), British musician and songwriter

Richardson, Samuel (1689–1761), English novelist

Rickles, Don (b. 1926), American comedian and actor

Rinehart, Mary Roberts (1876–1958), American novelist

Rivers, Joan (b. 1933), American comedian

Reagan, Ronald (1911–2004), fortieth U.S. president

Robbins, Harold (1916–1997), American novelist

Rock, Chris (b. 1966), American comedian and actor

Rogers, Will (1879–1935), American humorist

Roosevelt, Eleanor (1884–1962), American First Lady and diplomat

Roosevelt, Franklin Delano (1882–1945), thirty-second U.S. president

Roosevelt, Theodore (1858–1919), twenty-sixth U.S. president

Rostand, Edmond (1868–1918), French poet and dramatist
Ruskin, John (1819–1900), British art critic
Russell, Bertrand (1872–1970), British philosopher and mathematician
Sahl, Mort (b. 1927), American comedian
Sand, George pseudonym of Amandine Aurore Lucie Dupin, baronne Dudevant (1804–76), French novelist
Sandburg, Carl (1878–1967), American biographer and poet
Saint-Saens, Camille (1835–1921), French composer
Scholes, Percy A. (1877–1958), British music critic
Scott, Sir Walter (1771–1832), Scottish novelist and poet
Shakespeare, William (1564–1616), British dramatist
Shaw, George Bernard (1856–1950), Irish dramatist and critic
Shaw, Henry Wheeler, see Billings, Josh
Sheed, Wilfred (b. 1930), American writer
Shelley, Percy Bysshe (1792–1822), English poet
Sheridan , Richard Brinsley (1751–1816), British playwright and politician
Simon, John (b. 1925), American theater, film, and book critic
Sitwell, Dame Edith (1887–1964), English poet and critic
Skelton, Red (1913–1997), American comedian
Snow, C. P. (1905–1980), English author
Stein, Gertrude (1874–1946), American experimental writer
Stevenson, Robert Louis (1850–1894), British novelist

Stone, Sharon (b. 1958), American actress

Streisand, Barbra (b. 1942), American singer and actress

Strong, George Templeton (1856–1948), American composer

Swift, Jonathan (1667–1745), British writer and satirist

Swinburne, Algernon Charles (1837–1909), English poet

Taft, William Howard (1857–1930), twenty-seventh U.S. president

Talleyrand-Perigord, Charles-Maurice de (1754–1838), French statesman

Taylor, Elizabeth (b. 1928), Anglo-American actress

Tchaikovsky, Pyotr Illyich (1840–1893), Russian composer

Tennyson, Alfred (1809–1892), British poet

Thatcher, Margaret (b. 1925), British prime minister

Theroux, Paul (b. 1941), American travel author and journalist

Thomas, Dylan (1914–1953), Welsh poet

Thompson, Hunter S. (1939–2005), American writer

Thoreau, Henry David (1817–1862), American writer and philosopher

Thurber, James (1894–1961), American humorist

Todd, Michael (1907–1958), American producer

Tolstoy, Leo, Count (1828–1910), Russian novelist

Toscanini, Arturo (1867–1957), Italian-American orchestral conductor

Toynbee, Arnold (1852–1883), English economic historian, philosopher, and reformer

Trollope, Anthony (1815–1882), British novelist

Truman, Harry S. (1884–1972), thirty-third U.S. president

Twain, Mark, pen name of Samuel L. Clemens (1835–1910), American humorist and author

Van Dyke, Henry (1852–1933), American clergyman and author

Vidal, Gore (b. 1929), American writer

Voltaire, pen name of François-Marie de Arouet (1694–1778), French philosopher and author

Wagner, Richard (1813–1830), German composer

Waits, Tom (b. 1949), American musician and songwriter

Walpole, Horace (1717–1797), British author

Warhol, Andy (1928–1987), American pop artist

Washington, George (1732–1799), first U.S. president

Waugh, Evelyn (1903–1966), English writer

Webster, Daniel (1782–1852), American congressman

Wells, H. G. (1866–1946), British author

Welles, Orson (1915–1985), American film and stage actor and director

Wesley, John (1703–1791), British religious leader

Whistler, James Abbott McNeill (1834–1903), American artist

White, William Allen (1868–1944), American newspaper editor and writer

Whitman, Walt (1819–1892), American poet

Wilde, Oscar (1854–1900), Irish dramatist

Wilder, Billy (1906–2002), Austrian-American film director

Wilding, Michael (1912–1979), British actor

Wilhelm II (1859–1941), German emperor

Will, George F. (b. 1941), American political journalist

Williams, Robin (b. 1952), American actor and comedian

Wilson, Edmund (1895–1972), American critic and author

Wilson, Woodrow (1856–1924), twenty-eighth U.S. president

Wodehouse, P. G. (1881–1975), English-American novelist

Woods, Tiger (b. 1975), American golfer

Woolf, Virginia (1882–1941), English novelist and essayist

Woollcott, Alexander (1887–1943), American drama critic and journalist

Wright, Steven (b. 1955), American comedian

Yeats, William Butler (1865–1939), Irish poet

Youngman, Henny (1906–1998), American comedian